so for your dreams

INTUITION IS THE WINDOW TO THE KNOWING

To George
master, teacher, wise man,
mentor, and angel,
who taught me
to trust my intuition.

To Mariah,
my precious daughter,
who used her intuition
to choose me as her mom.

Fire Up Your Intuition!

A Journey to the Knowing

by
Donna Hartley

Fire Up Your Intuition: A Journey to the Knowing

By Donna Hartley

1. Body, Mind & Spirit : Spirituality - General 2. Body, Mind & Spirit : Healing - General 3. Biography & Autobiography : Personal Memoirs

ISBN: 978-1-935953-16-6

Cover design by Lewis Agrell

Printed in the United States of America

Authority Publishing

11230 Gold Express Dr. #310-413

Gold River, CA 95670

800-877-1097

www.AuthorityPublishing.com

Fire Up Series

In these uncertain times, the human spirit yearns for hope and enlightenment so each of us may survive and thrive. The **Fire Up** series recounts a compelling true-life journey, delivering timely inspiration along with timeless wisdom. Donna Hartley is crowned Miss Hawaii and her attention is captured by a kind and patient soul, George, who mysteriously prophesies that her success is paved with learning lessons. He relates to her in storytelling form that Donna must survive three life-threatening events if she is to fulfill her destiny. Is George a wise man, a mentor, an angel, or all three?

Fire Up Your Life! recounts Donna's near-death experience in a DC-10 plane crash at Los Angeles International Airport, which occurs directly after she expresses her desire to change her life or die. Trapped in the flaming inferno, she receives a mysterious message questioning her actions on earth. She wills herself to survive and is the last passenger out of her section of the aircraft. With the steadfast help of her teacher George, the reluctant student Donna begins a journey of spiritual transformation committing herself to change her fearful and unhealthy lifestyle. Her first assignment is to fight for improved airline safety regulations. Next, she must conquer her destructive relationships with men. Moreover, to become a successful entrepreneur she must master her fears.

Fire Up Your Intuition! finds Donna distraught in an emotional and financial crisis. George unexpectedly appears and bestows on her five mysterious envelopes that hold a 30-day assignment that he calls "the gift of intuition." The banter and discussion continue between student and teacher as Donna works to acquire insight into her own intuitive awareness. Her faithful Himalayan cat Sheba is by her side as Donna follows George's program step by step to learn to trust her feelings and act upon them to master *the knowing*. George predicts that when she completes her assignment, her dream to adopt a daughter will come true.

Fire Up Your Healing! narrates the sometimes rocky path on the passage toward family forgiveness leading to emotional maturity and the strength to heal. Donna travels from the tragic confines of her mother's post-stroke nursing home to the somber quarters of the judge empowered with deciding the fate for the bitter court battle in which her stepmother has embroiled Donna and her brother upon their father's death. George adamantly advises her to release her anger in order to survive. Could she forgive the alcoholism, the violence, and the indifference? This skill is now essential if she is to survive her stage III melanoma. But can she forgive herself and live to raise her six-year-old daughter? George mystically appears in the hospital to give Donna a shot of spiritual adrenalin and the courage to face down the deadly disease.

Fire Up Your Heart! begins at the gravesite of her stepdad as a heartbroken Donna deals with the eleventh death of family and friends in the past few years. Her nagging intuition forces her to consult a heart specialist and the prognosis is her worst fear: she must have immediate open-heart surgery to replace her failing aortic valve. Her daughter Mariah, now age ten, is the driving force to help her live. Donna's friends rally to lend her support for the delicate surgery scheduled for **March 1**, the same date of her plane crash and melanoma diagnosis. What are those chances? Donna must summon all her strength and hard-won wisdom to survive. Will George spiritually guide her through this life-threatening operation? Has Donna learned her lessons so she can cheat death for the third time?

Acknowledgements

To Jeanne Snoza, whose words of wisdom in the middle of the night gave me the will to believe. Thanks for being there for me.

To Joan Roelke, whose patience on re-writes was beyond amazing.

To Colleen Dunstan or "Cousin Colleen," whose insistence gave me the courage to pass on the knowledge of intuition I was given.

To Andrea Hurst, whose polishing edits enlightened me on how the book could help more people.

To Angela Booras, my neighbor, who became my sounding board on everything from raising kids to food, family issues, helping in the schools, and who just plain listened to me complain. Girlfriend and neighbor, you are an angel.

To Jacki Willette, whose knowledge on the computer brought this book to fulfillment.

Table of Contents

Part I
Five Levels

Chapter One
A Call for Help

There are no accidents
Everything happens for a reason

Tahoe City was awash with the crimson and gold colors of fall.
Tranquil Lake Tahoe shimmered like fine blue porcelain beneath
a blazing sun. I steered my car into a parking space in front of the
quaint building that housed the local post office. Lacking door-to-
door mail delivery in our community, the post office was a hub where
locals socialized, gossiped, and discussed the weather.

I gathered up my purse and mail, hopped out of the car, and
stopped dead in my tracks. The urge to crawl under my car and hide
was overwhelming, but there I stood, paralyzed on wooden legs,
wide-eyed in shock. My breath caught in my throat as I flattened
myself against the car, begging the Universe to make me invisible.
The sight of my ex-boyfriend Matt, leaning in so close to the younger,
slimmer woman he had dumped me for, set my heart hammering
until I thought it would explode. I had spent my entire life trying to
be slender, and the mere sight of her slim figure had me sucking in

my stomach, wishing fifteen pounds would melt off me like butter.

Then my eyes caught and locked on the diamond-encrusted wedding band on her finger. I sagged beneath the grim recollection of the four years I had waited for a wedding ring that never materialized. After several agonizing minutes, the couple moved toward a brand-new SUV with two expensive mountain bikes hooked onto the back. As they drove off together, I watched in disgust, fighting back waves of nausea. *Donna, get it together. People are looking at you. Get it together now. He chose her. He moved on.* My emotions felt like a roller coaster ride.

When Matt and I were together I was enamored with his good looks and charm. I believed our relationship was destined for marriage. Foolishly, I had put him on the deed to my house. The house I loved and had worked so hard to buy. The first house I had ever owned. I was devastated when I realized I'd chosen a man who was self-serving. I yearned for marriage and a family, but his focus was different. I believed he would change over time. Matt became more distant and started leaving every weekend. When he returned he said that all he needed was a little space.

Then, one day, right after he left, I heard a flirtatious, sexy voice on his answering machine whispering that she couldn't wait for another exciting weekend with him to begin. When I confronted Matt the scene was ugly, filled with angry, spiteful words. I had to retain a lawyer to evict him. To make matters worse, I had to pay a fortune to get him off the deed. Secretly, my ex had kept a list of all the money he had spent on me over the four years we were together, including presents he had bought me, and now he wanted it all back. He also demanded reimbursement for house expenses he had paid while living with me, such as utility bills. When the settlement was finalized to remove him from the deed, I was left making my monthly mortgage payment and an additional payment to him as well, and that left me with nothing to live on.

I watched them drive away. Had my money bought her diamond ring, the new car, and the expensive mountain bikes? I would bet my last dollar on it. Even worse, the money I paid him was planned for adopting the child I longed to have.

All my life I always believed I would meet the man of my dreams and have a family, but my relationships never led to marriage. After Matt, and in my forties, I adjusted my plan and began considering adoption alone. Since Matt had drained me emotionally and financially, it seemed every hope of having the life I yearned for was gone. I made the last and final payment to him and I was broke. Would I have what it took to put the past behind me and move on?

Lost in a limbo of self-pity, while praying I'd see no one else I knew, I finally dragged myself into the post office, collected my bills, and returned to my car. Resisting the urge to sort through my mail, I threw it down on the seat beside me and turned the key in the ignition. The engine sputtered, then died. I tried again. *Come on, car. Please get me out of this parking lot. You're old. You need a tune-up, but please start, please.* It was all I could do to hold back the tears that threatened what little control I had left. Two tries later, the engine turned over and I fled for home.

The drive to my house was only two miles. If I hadn't been overwhelmed with humiliation, I would have noticed how breathtaking the view of Lake Tahoe was that day. The crystal-clear water resonated calm as the brilliant sunlight glistened on the magnificent mountains peaks. I shrunk in my seat and gripped the steering wheel as tightly as I could. After an eternity of five minutes, I pulled into my driveway nestled in the trees on a grassy slope overlooking the lake. Parking my car, I snatched up the stack of bills I could no longer ignore. Resting my head against the steering wheel, I collapsed into despair. I now stood to lose everything I'd worked so hard to acquire. The past few years consisted of long, six-day workweeks. I glanced toward my empty house, waves of loneliness washing over me.

Overcome with exhaustion and wanting nothing more than to lie down and sleep, I went inside. A sensation of weight and softness against my leg lifted the heaviness in my heart. My furry friend, confidant, and soul mate, my cat Sheba, greeted me with her soft-purring way of saying that I really wasn't alone, and that she was here to soothe my heartache. I reached down to reward her with maternal cuddling and she gave me her full attention, rolling over with her four paws in the air. The stunning markings of a blue-point Himalayan gave her a royal quality, and her huge blue eyes sparkled as she rose and puffed up her back, purring.

Glancing at the clock, I panicked, realizing my date was due to arrive in an hour. Friends had introduced me to a local contractor, thinking we might be a match. He seemed interesting and easy to talk to on the phone.

Quickly shoving the bills into a drawer beneath my work calendar; my stomach became queasy when I saw my light work schedule for the next few months. My cat continued to gaze up at me, her eyes bright and alert. "Sheba, I'm going on a date. Wish me luck. Who knows, maybe he'll like me," I said with a tremor in my voice.

Standing before the mirror in my bedroom, I tried on five outfits, and the last was the winner. This one matched my mood; black pants, black sweater, and a dark green leather jacket. The loose curls in my red hair seemed to be going in every direction. My fair Irish skin was blotchy, but a little extra makeup would cover up my flaws. My hazel eyes seemed dull. Some eyeliner would work wonders. Even so, doubt nagged at me. How would he think I looked?

In the dimly lit living room, I picked up a magazine and sat down to wait for Prince Charming to arrive. Okay, he was just a date, but I have an overactive imagination. After reading the same article three times, I thought music might be nice, and maybe I should ask if he wanted a glass of wine before we left. Searching in the fridge for a bottle, I found a Chardonnay of dubious quality.

I checked my watch; he was ten minutes late. Twenty minutes later, I had flipped through four magazines and still no date. I checked my hair and makeup in the mirror and then checked for messages. None. I re-stacked the magazines and pushed them aside. Thirty minutes of diversion had passed and still no date. After an hour, I stopped dreaming up excuses and began pacing the carpet, staring out the window, searching for headlights in the driveway. By now, I couldn't keep my eyes off the clock and my gut was telling me that he was a no-show.

Deflated, emotionally raw, and exposed, I leaned back against the sofa cushions and sobbed in hot, ragged gasps. Only the fear of scaring Sheba held back the wails of sorrow and anger that raged inside me. I don't know how long I sat in a stupor crying, feeling like a cement truck had unloaded its cargo on my head. Trembling and spent, I struggled to gain control of myself by listening to the soulful music coming through the stereo speakers.

Stumbling toward my bedroom I grabbed tissues and fell backward onto my bed. Sheba, my faithful buddy, followed behind. She jumped up on the comforter and gently put one paw and then the other on my chest. Tears streamed down my face as she glared at me. It was as if she was looking straight into my soul. Sheba and I had been through plenty together—from days of pure joy and laughter in the backyard to the final struggles of unforgettable fights with the ex-boyfriend, to the marketing director who stole from me, to the self-doubt and loathing I have often battled. My body shook as my emotions crashed. Sheba wouldn't budge. I propped up my head on a pillow and looked intently at her. She was communicating a telepathic message. *Mom, stop it.* Time stood still and neither one of us moved. Sheba seemed to be pleading with me to conquer this pattern.

"Okay, you win," I mumbled through a stuffy nose. "I'll get my journal and work out my problems on paper. Happy now?" Leaning

over to my night stand I pulled out my thick, worn journal from the
top drawer. Sheba slid off my chest and snuggled against my waist.

Journal
A Call for Help

My life, yes ... my life seems to be helter-skelter again. I thought I
had taken a different path and I was on track, but old emotions keep
coming up and sabotaging my happiness. As my cat insisted, I have to
stop going two steps forward and one back. Weird, I feel like someone
is in the room, but of course there is no one here. So maybe I am
losing it. Wow, I have that strong feeling someone is here again.

All right, let's sort this out. I left home from Bethlehem,
Pennsylvania right after high school to change the pattern in my life.
The alcoholism and violence in my family kept me off balance. So, I
went to the University of Montana for two cold years and then off to
the University of Hawaii to graduate. Sold pots and pans to survive
while earning my college degree. Yep, loved it there and even won the
title of Miss Hawaii. Next stop: Hollywood and eight terrible years of
struggling to make my mark as an actress. I was lied to, cheated on,
and thrown away for the next pretty face.

Finally, the culmination was being the last survivor from the rear
section of a fiery DC-10 plane accident at Los Angeles International
Airport. That's when it all changed. I looked at life differently. With
guidance from George, my mentor, I faced my self-sabotaging beliefs,
and overcame bulimia and thoughts of suicide. George and I had lots
and lots of conversations and yes, he insisted I awaken my spiritual
awareness if I was going to fulfill my destiny. It has been fifteen years
since the plane crash and I expected my life to be different by now.
I did the work, but so what ... George, you said you would teach me
about intuition, but you haven't. George, you broke your promise. If I

really knew how to trust my intuition I would not be in this financial and emotional mess. I need help. Please, please, I'm begging for help.

When the student is ready
the teacher will appear

Chapter Two

It Is Time

**We're all partners on this earth
to help each other learn and grow**

I shifted in the bed, trying to shut out the sound. *Wha ... what's that noise?* My head was throbbing. My back ached. *Stop that ringing.* I focused one eye on my digital clock. Was it five-thirty in the morning? Morning; it was morning—where had the night gone? I still had my clothes on and my sweater was twisted around me. My journal was on the bed and a box of tissue was right next to my head. Reaching awkwardly across the bed, I rummaged for the phone. "Hullo."

My old friend and mentor's chipper voice resonated over the line like he'd been awake for hours. "Good morning, Partner. Sounds like I woke you up."

I leaned on my forearm. "George! Where are you? Do you know it's five-thirty?" I yawned. "Of course you do. You woke me up." Shaking my head, I tried to make sense of what I was saying.

"Partner, rise and shine. You have some learning to do," he said.

"So where are you? What time zone are you in?"

He chuckled. "I'm in Incline Village. Do you know where that is?"

I bolted straight up in bed. "Are you really in Tahoe?"

"I really am. I had a meeting with a new client here. I decided to take another day before flying back home to Oklahoma and knew it was time for us to talk."

I squealed, "George, you're here and I need you! How do you always know to show up at the right time?"

"You know when you know, Donna," he said gently.

My throat tightened and I managed to say, "I'm in nose-dive mode ... again."

"Well then, I guess it's a good thing I decided to stay an extra day. See Donna, it's time."

"Time—what do you mean time? For what?" I asked.

"I promised that when the time was right I would teach you the gift of intuition. Today is the day."

"But George," I protested. "Today is not a good day. I feel like ..."

He interrupted, "You feel like you have nothing left. That's why it is the perfect day, because you are willing to listen and change. Your walls of resistance are down."

"But you don't ..."

"No buts, Partner, here's my idea. You've been lecturing me about crawdad fishing for years. Let's do that first thing and then we'll talk. I'm at the Hyatt, so come pick me up with some hot coffee."

"I'm barely awake, but I'm moving now," I said as I stood up.

"By the time you get here, you'll be wide awake. How long?"

"Give me thirty minutes, George, and I'll be out in front of the hotel with your blooming black coffee."

Chapter Three

Think It

*Become a master of life
not a passive participant*

Sunrise at Lake Tahoe was breathtaking. The air was silky fresh
and an alpenglow reflected on windswept mountains dappled with
giant pine, spruce, and cedar trees. A spectrum of color swept the
sky, rolling up from smoky amethyst to red-orange and bubble-gum-
pink. My gaze wandered to the dazzling clear lake and I thought how
strange it was to be surrounded by such majestic beauty, and yet to
be agonizing over my life. I was scared, paralyzed to act because my
resources were shaky.

As George and I strolled down the long, wooden pier extending
from the shore out over the water, my mind was going round and
round like a luggage carousel. I had a boatload of questions to ask
him, but he firmly proclaimed that first on the agenda was crawdad
fishing, and questions could come later.

What was our relationship, anyway? The first time I met George I
thought he was some kind of nut. Now I regard him as a man of great

insight and mystical knowledge. As George would say, "Don't judge a book by its cover." I remember him standing in the ballroom at the Miss Hawaii pageant in a gaudy flowered Hawaiian shirt, with his brown pipe and the scent of cherry tobacco surrounding him. I was flying high because I had just won the title of Miss Hawaii on the fifth attempt. He insisted we meet for breakfast. Through a set of uncanny circumstances, I actually met him the next morning, which was the first of hundreds of breakfasts to follow. My focus was on discussing how I would get money and a man, which he nicknamed M & M. On the other hand, George's emphasis was on helping me understand how to develop my spiritual insight. There was a higher source I needed to tap into before I could move with the flow of life. I was the resistant student; George was the patient teacher. He proclaimed he was assigned to watch over me. He always had a twinkle in his eye when he questioned what had he done in another lifetime to deserve this assignment.

He embodied the essence of an Oklahoma bumpkin with his pear-shaped body, wispy brown hair, glasses, and constant companion: his pipe. I would say to him that I thought his old, sage wisdom came from smoking his pipe. He'd chuckle and say, "There's probably some truth to that." George never ceased to amaze me because he would show up when I was in need. How did he know?

Believe in miracles
They happen when you are ready

Bundled in sweatshirts for the chilly morning, we inhaled the fresh, crisp air. Our footsteps echoed on the wooden planks. I toted a red plastic pail stuffed with turkey and salami for bait, and a plastic baggie of small rocks to use for sinkers. George carried our folding chairs and shouldered the two stick poles I had threaded with kitchen string. Several times I'd expressed to George how much I enjoyed crawdad fishing. The freshwater runt of the lobster family is a tasty delicacy, and catching them is a favorite Lake Tahoe pastime.

At this early hour the pier was deserted except for George and me. As we began to set up our gear, I saw George straighten up and cast a faraway look down the narrow strip of sandy beach. My eyes followed the path of his gaze to a fit-looking man I judged to be about forty. He bent down to remove his shoes. Wearing only shorts and a T-shirt, he waded into the water, staring trance-like across the lake.

"George, the water is freezing."

He hushed me. The man waded further into the water. At this time of year, Lake Tahoe was icy cold, and hypothermia could set in within minutes.

"He could freeze to death!" I stated as my voice escalated.

I gasped and brought my hand to my mouth. I realized the man was walking the same self-destructive path I had walked years ago. I flashed back to being seated aboard the Continental DC-10 taking off from Los Angeles. I had been on my way to the islands to emcee the Miss Hawaii pageant. Upon takeoff, my worst nightmare came true. At 167 miles per hour the plane blew three tires, smashed a tilted wing into the tarmac, and shattered. Terror invaded my body. When the plane exploded I knew I was going to die. I wanted to die. I felt my life was a sham as a Hollywood actress. The Universe had other ideas for me. Miraculously, I made my way through the flames and hordes of pushing, panicking passengers to the emergency exit. I leapt out the door and slid down the escape chute. As I landed on the tarmac and lurched to my feet, the evacuation chute burst into flames.

Shifting my head, I stared at the man and then looked back at George. "What does he think he's doing?" I implored, yanking off my sneakers. "I'm going after him."

"Be still and stay right where you are," George ordered. Concentrating intensely, he slowly inhaled and exhaled as he focused on the man.

A part of me wanted to scream at the stranger, "Stop. Please stop!" When I opened my mouth the only sound that came out was a useless gurgle. My eyes darted back and forth between George and the stranger, compelled to watch this drama play itself out.

The man was now up to his waist in the freezing water. He never paused or reacted to the cold, or even glanced our way, but he repeatedly looked back at the beach, as though agonizing over his decision. Ramrod-stiff, George maintained his focus, perspiration dampening his forehead and eyes glowing intently.

When the man reached chest-high water, he shivered and turned his head toward the end of the pier where George and I stood. None of us moved. The man slowly nodded and wrapped his arms around himself, suddenly aware that he was shivering from the cold. Mercifully, he turned and began wading back to the beach.

I glanced at George. His features had relaxed and he looked like his old self again.

"That was incredible. It's like something made him stop and turn around. Did you communicate with him? Did you tell him to stop?"

George held up his hand, peering over his fogged glasses. "Wait."

By the time the bedraggled-looking man had reached the end of the pier, he was shaking violently and his lips had a bluish cast to them. His eyes were bloodshot, wet with tears, and haunted by deep sadness. He closed his eyes for several seconds, then opened them and stared at George.

George spoke. "You need to see another doctor—a specialist who will provide a new course of treatment. Now, let's get you home and into some dry clothes. You will see your children grow up."

Tears formed in the corners of the man's eyes. "Thank you," he murmured. "My car is parked at the top of the hill." Then he turned and walked away.

I gazed up at George and blubbered, "We need to help him to his car and makes sure he gets home."

"No. Better he does it himself. Don't worry, he learned valuable insight, and it will mean more in the long run if he does it on his own."

Stunned from the whole experience, I realized how fortunate I was to witness such an alarming yet uplifting experience. For a simple guy from Oklahoma, George was the most complicated man I'd ever met. He was a crisis intermediary and could summon up answers to questions that were larger than everyday life.

After watching the attempted suicide, I pondered the threads in my own life that were unraveling. Sometimes I could patch things up, and other times the big, gaping holes in the fabric of my life seemed too huge to stitch together.

"I sense you want to know more about what happened," George quickly said. "By the end of the day you will have greater knowledge."

"What did happen here?"

"There a few basic reasons why people don't wish to live any longer; relationship, finance, and health problems top the list."

I nodded, thinking of my own thoughts of suicide. I softly said, "I know."

"Telepathically I picked up on his fear. It was his health. What I did was interrupt his limited thinking. He thought he would become a burden to his family and this was the only way out. I've spent years in meditation and studying in order to be able to do this."

"George, this is amazing stuff. One minute we're looking for crawdads and then this man ..."

"What I did was help him to stop and look at his situation differently. I was here to help him re-align his thinking."

"Will we see him again?"

George paused, that far away look in his eyes, and said, "No."

"Is he going to be all right?"

"He'll be fine."

"But ..."

"Later, you'll understand more. For now, let's see what this crawdad business is all about," George said, peering down at the clear water. "I'm darned anxious to catch some."

"Uh-huh. You don't say," I said, still wanting more explanation about what had just happened.

He turned to me with a gleam in his eyes. "Say, what's the best for bait? Salami or turkey?"

"Probably turkey," I mumbled, thinking how rare it was for George to ask a question requiring my knowledgeable answer.

"That's kind of bland. I think salami would be better."

I blinked several times. "How does a crawdad know the difference?"

He tilted his head to one side, thinking. "Well now, those little creatures have certain tastes like we do."

I grinned. "Okay. You take salami, I'll take turkey, and we'll see who catches the most crawdads."

After tying on our bait and adding rocks for sinkers, we cast our lines in the water and sat down to wait. George lit his pipe, puffing out billows of cherry tobacco smoke, and creaked back into his chair with the air of a man who had nothing but time on his hands.

With my usual lack of patience, I pulled up my string every few minutes to see if I had caught anything. Checking once again, I was annoyed to see that the creatures had snatched my bait.

Sensing a tug on my pole, I quickly pulled up. The crawdad was hanging on the end of the string for dear life. I had him out of the water and headed for the bucket when the little son of a gun let go and dropped back into the lake.

"Did you see that, George?" I stared glumly down at the water. "I almost had that little guy but he got away."

George glanced over at me and commented, "You need to stay focused until the crawdad is in the bucket. As usual, you are rushing ahead of yourself."

After George had caught his fourth crawdad, I grumbled, "I don't get it. Turkey usually works. I caught two of them last month in half the time with the exact same bait. Now this morning, every time I pull up on my pole, they get away. It's not like I haven't done this before." I peered into the pail and exclaimed, "You're catching all the crawdads, George. Hey. Hold on. I bet I know the problem. I'm fishing on the wrong side of the pier."

George cranked a hand around like a director waving for action. "You have to be still, not chatter so much, and don't keep checking your line all the time. Fishing is a quiet sport. Don't force the issue. Let the crawdads come to you." He labored his portly self out of the chair and stood up. "Here now, let's switch chairs. You take my bait and I'll take yours. Don't let your impatience get the best of you, Partner, and the crawdads will come to you," he said confidently.

Rubbing my hands together, I said, "Now I'll catch them." There he was, calling me Partner again. Maybe if I asked why, I'd get him talking. *Yes, talk. That's what I really wanted to do. Talk.* "George, why do you call me Partner?"

He smiled. "Because we all work together on this planet."

That prompted me to remember when he told me he'd been assigned twelve people to look after, including myself, who needed extra help. George is what I would call a spiritually advanced soul, or what some others would call an "old soul." With his wisdom he provides counsel to each of us, but will not intervene to spare any one of us our learning lessons by telling us what to do. As blessed as I was to have George in my life, nothing frustrated me more than when he began one of his parables, otherwise known as a Georgeism, when all I wanted was a straight answer. He was a real stickler for making sure everyone was accountable for their own choices. There were no free passes with George!

After half an hour, he had caught a total of nine crawdads to my one.

I frowned down into the pail at the squirmy little creatures. "So, what is the best bait—turkey or salami?"

George emptied his pipe, gently tapping it on the wooden pier piling. "It has nothing to do with the salami or the turkey. Patience is like a powerful magnet. It attracts certain things to you. Crawdad fishing is a lot like life. It's a process. You clear your mind, get your thoughts centered on what you want, and send out the energy. You've heard that old saying 'patience of Job'? It's perseverance that creates results."

I mumbled, "You mean I should think crawdads onto my line? Think ... think ... is that what you did with the man standing in water up to his chest? You sent out your energy and communicated with him? Did you think him to stop?"

George laid his charmed fishing pole aside and rubbed his hands together to warm them. "You might say that. He is a good man who needed some help. I was destined to be here for him. Now, back to what I was saying. There is a specific learning lesson in crawdad fishing. Can you tell me what it is?"

"I don't know. Salami works better than turkey? All right then, turkey works better than salami."

George glanced at me over the top of his glasses and gave me one of his looks. "More than that. The lesson here is for you to set your purpose, then **think it**, and believe it will happen."

He chuckled. "People aren't successful because they get a break or carry a lucky charm in their pocket. They must first take the steps and then climb up each level to master their existence."

I pondered over his words. Where was all this going? "Steps? Levels? This isn't making sense to me."

"Yup," he said with an amused look, and continued as if he hadn't heard me. "I've been sensing that your life hasn't been flowing smoothly for you, as if you're in an anxious stall pattern."

I agreed by shaking my head.

"I'm only here for the day, but sharing the five levels of awareness will help you with your predicament. Becoming more aware of the who, what, when, and why of your life will position you to be more in tune with your emotions, so there aren't so many dramatic peaks and sinking valleys. It takes meditation to quiet your mind and help heighten your intuition. The first level is **think it**. So to put it simply, you've got some work to do, Partner," George drawled.

"What exactly do you mean?"

George regarded me from behind his glasses. "I mean that it's time to develop your spiritual awareness. Patience is a key ingredient. I know you want it all now, but these things take time to cultivate."

Just being with George made me feel better. What he said was absolutely on target, but I felt inadequate and a bit scared.

"Mr. Mentor, at this moment, I don't feel I can hold myself together long enough to progress through any level."

"That's because you're focusing on your failures. Let's get back to level one, **think it.** Decide what it is you want to draw to yourself. After you do that, start thinking about it morning, noon, and night. Keep it at the front of your mind and after a while you'll notice results."

Open your eyes
to all possibilities

"As you grow more in tune with your intuition it will guide you to a balanced life. Your goal is to be more self-assured."

George pointed down at the pail, then picked it up and released the crawdads into the lake. "Go on, little fellas, time for you to go back home."

A cool breeze fluttered George's thinning hair and a knowing, thoughtful expression appeared on his face as he spoke. "Donna, before I even arrived here in Tahoe, I sensed that you were struggling, so I extended my stay. When I called this morning, I could hear the depression in your voice. You can't expect to have a brilliant future with your emotions bouncing up and down like a pogo stick."

I cleared my throat nervously. "I'm skydiving with no parachute."

George let loose a deep belly laugh. "The Universe is saying you need to re-program yourself. Like a computer. It isn't guaranteed to work right forever. It may crash from time to time and have to be fixed. Well, we've got some fixing to do, and I'm happy to be here. It's not hard to see that you're stuck and going nowhere. We need to get you unstuck, fired up, and back on track, Partner."

I looked up, rolling my eyes. "It's going to take more than a day, George."

"Consider the plane crash. It only took thirty seconds for you to change. It's all up to you; it can take thirty seconds, thirty minutes, thirty days, or thirty years. It's your choice."

The early sun cast its powerful rays on the water and I reached for my dark glasses. George's concept was intriguing. I turned to him. "You're saying I can change my outlook, my future, by altering the way I think? Seems I've tried that a few times before and I always slip back into the same old self-defeating patterns. I promised myself after the plane crash I'd never fall into those self-destructive beliefs again."

George nodded in understanding.

I thought for a moment, then continued, "I have drawn some wonderful things to me—my house, my speaking career, living in Tahoe, and even my cat. Still, I'm that pogo stick you mentioned bouncing out of control. I absolutely fell apart when I ran into my ex-boyfriend and his young wife yesterday. Here I am struggling to pay my bills, and there they are living the high life on my money." I looked at George pleadingly. "Do you really think I have what it takes to start over again?"

He nodded. "I do. Unless it's your health or your family, you don't need to lose sleep. Money or no money, that's a temporary state you can change. There truly is a higher power, and now is the time to align yourself with its presence and begin doing your work." George waved an index finger at me to emphasize his point. "I'm telling you it's worth the effort to change and create the life you want."

"But George ..."

"It's all tied into your thoughts and actions. When you focus on negativity, you get negativity in return. When you focus on the positive, you get positive results."

"Now that makes some sense. I have been focusing on the negative."

A smile formed on his lips. "Let's back up to this morning. When you didn't catch any crawdads, you started a cycle of blaming. First you blamed the turkey, then the salami, then the crawdads, and finally, where you were sitting. What you should have been thinking all along was that you could catch lots of these little critters."

I shook my head. "It isn't that simple. You can't change your life by thinking. If that were the case, everyone would be happy and successful."

"That's the problem, Partner. Every human has the promise and the means, but some refuse to take the steps needed to center their thoughts and live creative lives. They, like you, find it easier to be a victim."

I shrugged my shoulders.

"There's no mystery, Donna. I'm putting you on a path you can follow. Levels are something everyone can achieve."

"What you really mean is that you're going to level with me."

He chuckled. "Exactly. I'll keep you busy, Partner."

I drew in a deep breath, let it out, and said, "Okay. I always give you a hard time when I have to change."

"You certainly do. Whether you want to believe it or not, you have been learning. You've temporarily gotten yourself stuck in negative thinking. I'm here to get you back on your higher path."

"Thank you. I'm so glad you showed up."

"Look at it this way," he continued. "With a little effort and attention you can alter your life physically, emotionally, mentally, and spiritually. You already know about the external senses like sight, sound, smell, touch, and taste. Opening up to your intuition is learning to use your internal senses."

I nodded vaguely. "Maybe I got overlooked in that department."

"Take my word for it. You own them. Instead of being tangible, your internal senses are awareness, feelings, sensations, or quick thoughts. Intuition is a multi-sensory perception that can be developed into what I call *the knowing*."

George's excitement shone through his eyes. "A positive viewpoint attracts powerful energy."

My stubborn grey matter tried to digest what he was saying. "You make it sound so simple, George, but it's not that easy."

A spontaneous chuckle erupted from him. "Like thinking you didn't catch crawdads because you didn't have the right bait? You were so negative this morning you couldn't even attract a little crawdad into your life. What you thought is what you got. An important part of getting in tune with yourself is paying close attention to what you think because your thoughts create your reality."

"George, I'm trying but ... I think I am ..."

"Donna, don't kid yourself; it takes more than wanting it to be. You've got to work on your belief system every day and on many levels. Think and act to manifest the life you want."

I smiled up at him. "You never throw in the towel, do you? Never give up. All these years of putting up with me, guiding me, and you've never lost patience."

Tears welled in my eyes. "You are special, George. I know I have more lessons to learn, and some to re-learn. The first was the plane crash and then testifying to change safety regulations. What's next?"

George nodded. "Donna, you have two more major turning points, and if you survive, you will help a lot of people. We learn from both pleasant and painful experiences. What you truly think on the inside is what's reflected to the Universe. That's all I'm going to say on this subject. Don't ask me any more questions now."

"But I need to know if ..."

"There are no rights and no wrongs—only learning lessons." George trudged along, continuing with his straight talk as we climbed off the pier onto the damp sand. "Your mission is to learn more about who you are," he said, pointing at his heart, "and your true purpose. Go to the first level and **think it**. Eliminate your doubt. In everything you think about, be positive."

Breathlessly forging up the hill carrying the beach chairs, he continued, "My lesson is that I need to exercise more often. Whew! I'm tired. Exercise is not my favorite thing." He glanced my way. "So Partner, before we leave this paradise, or I run completely out of wind, tell me what insights you've learned this morning."

What did I learn ... what did I learn ... my mind was blank. Then I turned to him and exclaimed excitedly, "What I think is what I draw to myself."

George grinned. "Couldn't have said it better myself. Now that we've got that out of the way, I could use another hot cup of coffee. How about surprising me with the locals' favorite coffee shop?"

I gave him a thumbs up sign. "But what comes next? What's the next level about? Can we talk on the way? I have a few zillion more questions to ask. Gimme a hint, gimme a hint. What's the next level?"

George laughed. "All right ... hmm. Level two is happiness and love all rolled into one. Now, that's all I'm going to say. Feed me first; answers later."

You can't expect a first grader
to do twelfth grade homework
Take one step at a time

Chapter Four
Feel It

When the time is right
you will attract the answer

Warm sunlight cast a cheery golden glow into the busy little coffee shop. The scents of fresh-baked pastry and hot brewed coffee made my stomach growl for food. George and I sat down at a small wrought iron table by the window overlooking the lake. He commandeered a copy of the local paper and began poring over the headlines. I was too wound up to read the newspaper, so I glanced around to see if anyone I knew was there. Smiling, I waved at a friend from my exercise class. At the next table, a despondent-looking couple, young but stylish, sat drinking coffee and staring indifferently out the window.

I quickly glanced away. "George, what are you going to have to eat? George, George, earth to moon. What's level two?"

He peered over the top of his newspaper and let out a sigh before putting down his paper. "Okay, I'll tell you about the next level."

I opened my mouth to ask yet another question, but George put up his hand to keep me at bay and said, "Level two is **feel it**. That's all I'm going to say until I get my coffee and a cinnamon roll."

"All right. Have it your way. You know they have bagels, apple turnovers, scones—all kinds of pastries that melt in your mouth, and lattés to die for."

He squinted at the espresso machines hissing out steaming brews and frothed milk. "Do you drink that stuff or just listen to it?"

Laughing, I pointed at the menu behind the coffee bar. "Now, what are you going to have?"

"Black coffee and a cinnamon roll."

I studied him for a moment. "That's it? Really?"

"Yup. Keep it simple."

"Boring, but if you change your mind, I'll share my raspberry scone with you."

It wasn't easy for me, nibbling away and trying to keep quiet while George read. I was particularly eager to talk about this level two.

Suddenly a jarring voice at the next table declared, "Even in a peaceful place like this, you ignore me. All you did yesterday was phone your office every half hour. I thought we could do something together for a change." The unhappy woman at the next table was spitting out words the way a snake spits venom. Sitting up straighter in my chair, I half-expected George to put his paper down, but he didn't.

The well-groomed man sitting across from her retorted, "How do you think I'm paying for this stupid trip? It was your idea, not mine. The timing couldn't have been worse. I should be at the office right now, not sitting in some resort being chewed out by you."

"You're always at the office. We never go anywhere together anymore. All you care about is work," she responded in a quavering voice. "I was hoping this trip might help get our relationship back on track, but it's falling apart. Or are you too busy working to even notice?"

"You bet I am. You like to eat out, shop, and spend money like it grows on trees. Cook much at home? All I get is trendy restaurant take-out. It's no wonder I stay at work. And by the way," he said maliciously, "have another croissant. Forget about the calories."

Stealing a quick glance at the woman, I saw that her face was tight, lips drained of color, and she was struggling to maintain control. After a few tense moments, she threw down her napkin and stood up so abruptly that her chair crashed to the floor. "I'm out of here. The next plane," she growled through clenched teeth. Storming out the door, she never glanced back as her husband jumped up to follow after her, shaking his reddening face in fury.

George carefully folded his newspaper and gazed at me with a pained look on his face. "Two unhappy souls giving out negativity and receiving negativity. They're letting their anger overpower them. They should talk about what they're feeling with love and concern, not resentment."

I shook my head. "I don't know exactly how they feel, but I think I have something in common with them. Sometimes I don't feel loved and don't believe I'm worthy of love."

He took a sip of his coffee. "You first have to feel you are worthy of love. The idea is to love your creator and love yourself."

"I know it's possible to change, but ..."

"A whole bunch of folks think that a stylish car, a new house, or even an exotic vacation will bring them happiness. From what I heard, it wasn't what those two needed." He nodded at the door. "Unless they talk through their feelings, they will continue to be miserable."

I frowned. "How do you know if a relationship is right for you? Or, for that matter, how does anyone know what real love is?"

George pondered. "The answer isn't that simple. Some folks have the perfect mate all picked out—handsome, beautiful, rich, and so on. They allow their egos to dictate their choices and focus on superficial, rather than inner, beauty. Common values, that's what's important. If the man you marry doesn't accept you as the person you are, and you try to change solely for him, you're agreeing that the real you isn't good enough. Oh sure, we all need some fine-tuning, but if you don't love and respect yourself, how do you expect others to?"

Groaning, I nodded. "I'll never forget the time I went back to Pennsylvania for my class reunion. I didn't eat for three days so I could fit into a gorgeous little blue dress so tight I had to flip a coin to decide which single piece of lingerie I should wear underneath."

George rolled his eyes.

"I was looking hot. I had my hair and nails done, and even had a facial. Instead of telling me how great I looked, my mother bugged me because I didn't have a date. That got my Irish up and I went to the reunion alone, hell-bent on finding love. After an hour or so, I glanced across the room and saw this guy I was nuts about in high school, back when he wouldn't even give me the time of day."

George blinked a couple of times. "Did Mr. Dreamboat have a name?"

I giggled. "Joe, his name was Joe, with a long last name I could hardly pronounce. He took one look at me, and we ended up laughing and dancing the night away. All I could think was, boy oh boy, had I proved my mother wrong. There was someone who wanted me, and who cared if he worked at the sanitation landfill."

Behind his glasses, George's eyes widened. "You mean the dump?"

"Exactly, but they don't call it that nowadays."

"Well, at least he made an honest living."

"Wait until you hear the rest. I came back to Tahoe, and a while later Joe flew out here to see me. The first couple of days were so much fun sightseeing and driving around the lake. On the third day, we were in a 7-Eleven when a road work crew wearing orange jump suit uniforms walked in. While Joe was filling his coffee cup, he said, 'Yo baby, hey, that's what I wear to work.' I stared at him. At that moment I realized that our lifestyles and values were very different.

Besides, we lived on opposite ends of the country."

George nodded. "Partner, a real relationship takes time, and open honest communication. You'll know it's right when you share common values. With Joe, you didn't pay any attention to your values—only your hormones and proving your mother wrong." George gave me his spiritual teacher look. "That's what level two, **feel it**, is about: getting in touch with your true feelings."

Mulling over what George had said, I glanced back at the empty table where the couple had been, and recalled their bitter words. "Do you think those two will work it out? They said some mean things to each other."

"Well, divorce is not a subject I usually talk about." He gave a little sigh. "It depends on how truthful they are with themselves and each another. The young woman is not happy with herself and that has a lot to do with her insecurity. Plus, the husband needs to share his inner feelings. Remember, you have to love yourself before you can love someone else. You can't expect another person to make you feel good about yourself."

"On a lighter note, let me tell you what I learned today," he said, patting his belly. "Climbing up the hill from the pier this morning, I learned that walking is something I need to do more often, and God knows as much I love them, I have to cut down on the pastries."

He narrowed his gaze and shot me a look. "What insights have you gained?"

"Before I try to answer that, please help me understand something. Level one is **think it** and level two is **feel it**. When I heard that fighting couple saying such hurtful things, it made me realize how often I say negative things to myself."

"Keep in mind the difference between negative criticism and constructive feedback. Negative criticism has no redeeming value. Constructive criticism is a guide to improvement."

I smacked my hand on the table. "That's what's wrong with me.

Why I have no energy! I'm listening to my own negative messages instead of feeling that I am worthy."

"That's what I've been waiting to hear!" George beamed.

He snatched up his pipe. "That's the ticket, Partner. Let's head over to that Fanny Bridge you've told me about. My goal is to walk off my cinnamon roll and check out the trout."

"Sure, you'll enjoy Tahoe City even more on foot." George was already halfway out the door when I rose from my chair and trotted after him saying, "But what's level three?"

> ***Create your own happiness***
> ***Reach inward***
> ***for your true feelings***

Chapter Five

Visualize It

Begin by visualizing your
dreams in your mind

Walking through town, George slowly puffed on his pipe and blew out a wisp of cherry scent. "Great little place," he declared, "a whole lot different from where you lived in Los Angeles."

"That's an understatement," I said, laughing. "Living with the 24/7 traffic on Wilshire Boulevard was like living with a throbbing migraine headache. Life in Los Angeles was like riding a bull; I hung on until I was thrown off."

Steering him to the left I said, "Right there, that's Fanny Bridge."

He squinted his eyes at the stopped traffic. "You know, that's the first traffic light I've seen since we left the coffee shop."

"It's the first, last, and only."

As we neared the bridge, the local gulls soared effortlessly over the sluice gates. After reaching into my pocket for some bread crumbs I had gathered up from the coffee shop, I held them in my open hand. Tourists with cameras dangling from their necks were lined up on the bridge, hanging over the guardrail while watching the swirling water and feasting fish below.

George leaned over the railing and peered down at the plethora of trout swimming in the dam. "Who is Fanny and why did they name the bridge after her?" he asked, immersed in the fish action.

"Fanny wasn't a lady," I said, suppressing a giggle. "Fanny wasn't even a person."

"Really?" George straightened up and gawked around at the people hanging over the bridge with their posteriors pointed toward the traffic. He chuckled. "Oh yeah, I get it now. Fanny Bridge! That's great."

We watched the feeding frenzy of the gulls and then the trout. I tossed the crumbs into the air, and some made their way into the water. "This is where the lake fills the Truckee River."

George kept his eyes glued on the churning water. "Would you look at the size of that fish? They do grow them big in these waters." He inhaled deeply, then let his breath out slowly. "Smell that fresh air. You sure can feel powerful energy up here in the mountains. It's nature at work. People get so busy driving their cars and hopping on planes and trains, they don't take the time to see the beauty around them."

He nudged me with his elbow. "Hand over some of those crumbs, and let's hear about this Truckee River."

I emptied my other pocket into his hand, then pulled up the hood on my sweatshirt to ward off the chill. "Well, it's named after the town of Truckee, a booming, quaint town about twenty minutes north. The river follows Interstate 80 down the mountain and goes through Reno, Nevada. The Truckee River is a summer hot spot for river rafting and fly fishing." Checking my watch, I saw that it was almost eleven. George's flight was scheduled to leave at six o'clock. Curbing my impatience, I knew he'd move on when he was good and ready. Being a Taurus, he was as stubborn as a mule.

"So it all starts right here," George said, gazing around. "That's amazing. Yup, I can feel a lesson coming on." He framed a view of the town with his hands. "You know, if people hadn't seen this town, the bridge, the cobblestone walks and the park in their minds, these sites wouldn't be here."

He turned from the bridge and nodded. "It's time to explain level three."

"It's about time," I muttered.

George continued, ignoring my comment. "We've discussed **think it** and **feel it**, and next we have to see it ... or what you Californians call **visualize it**."

"Okay, I once understood and even practiced visualization stuff, but it slipped away, so please enlighten me with your words of wisdom. I can use some coaching."

Shivering, he rubbed his hands together. "Sure. Let's grab one of those benches over there on the bank."

George squinted his eyes. "This town was created because certain people had a vision. Some might call it a dream, others an inspiration. Whatever you label it, when you see something in your mind's eye, you are visualizing it. If folks didn't visualize, we wouldn't have bikes, cars, skyscrapers, computers, or even indoor plumbing. Someone formed a concept in his or her mind and then enriched that vision by giving it life."

A family ventured down to where we were sitting, and a young boy about ten years old, along with a girl a year or two younger, frolicked along the river bank tossing bread crumbs to the fish. The boy was zipped into a snappy blue Mickey Mouse jacket and the girl a bright red Minnie Mouse jacket. We watched them in silence until George let loose a belly laugh and remarked, "Even Mickey and Minnie are here visiting Tahoe."

He paused and I noticed a faraway expression drift into his eyes. "There wouldn't be a Mickey and Minnie Mouse if Walt Disney didn't have a vision and plenty of persistence. Yup, he was a showman way ahead of his time. He envisioned the first animated film with sound, and then made it happen. When other people saw only orange groves in Southern California, he saw an incredible entertainment park. In 1955, he founded Disneyland." George folded his arms over his chest, turned, and said, "But there's something else about Walt Disney you might not know."

I shrugged. "What's that?"

George gave a little snort. "Walt Disney went bankrupt many times before he saw his dream come true. In fact, Disneyland almost didn't become an enchanted paradise. Also, when he invested in swamp land in Florida, people laughed at him. They figured he would go belly-up, but his vision gave us Disney World and Epcot Center. Remember old Walt when life isn't going great. Don't give up on your dreams."

"Do I really have the energy to start over again for the umpteenth time?" I mentally ran through the list of bills in my desk drawer and heaved a sigh. "I'm alone and I'm not a mastermind like Walt Disney. I'm an ordinary person working to stay afloat."

"Partner, I want you to close your eyes and think of something you want."

"Okay, okay." I squeezed my eyes shut, and before long I had a vision that brought a wide smile to my lips. "I see before me a vision: brown eyes, wavy brown hair, handsome as all get out, six-pack abs, and the perfect biceps to squeeze me with."

His eyes sparkled with amusement. "Not exactly what I had in mind. A start, but let's put that one on hold for a while."

I pouted. "Darn it." A teenager skateboarding over the bridge while sipping a Slurpee caught my attention. "I know. I'm visualizing myself buying ten dollars' worth of lottery tickets. Then, I visualize those numbers being picked. I win five million dollars."

"I think I need a smoke," my wise sage said as he fumbled for his tobacco pouch.

"Hey, are you implying that I'm a cause that needs more than a little work?"

George flared a match while smiling. "Well said." He puffed until the smoke curled upward from his pipe and disappeared into the pines. "What I want you to do is relax. Uncross those arms, take a few deep breaths of this pure air, and loosen up."

I did as he asked, and this time, instead of pure air I got a big whiff of cherry tobacco. "George, I still think you get all your answers from that pipe." He cast me a glance. "The truth is that I spent all my money paying off my ex-boyfriend, business dropped off, I can't pay my mortgage, and I'm alone."

"It could be worse. Close your eyes again and this time imagine that the big calendar on your office wall is filled with speaking engagements. See yourself writing on the calendar. You're booked for one full year and heading straight into the next. Visualize. Whatever is happening in the world—war, violence, recession—does not prevent you from creating your own abundance."

I slouched. "Nothing has happened yet. How soon can I expect results?"

"What you want arrives only after you do the work. If you want a full calendar and financial abundance, you have to visualize it. First think it and draw it to you, like Walt Disney saw an amusement park where there were orange groves and swamp land. Feel the success, the energy. Then envision yourself answering the phone because the clients are calling you. Hook all the levels together. **Think it, feel it**, and **visualize it**."

My eyes popped open. George sounded so animated. He was something, waving his arms and tapping his feet. I squeezed my eyes shut, took a deep breath, and let myself relax. I anchored my thoughts on the calendar filling up, but other ideas kept interrupting. I breathed deeply and concentrated one more time. A passing car slammed on the brakes and I had to take a little peek.

"Keep working, Partner," I heard, "get centered and forget about what's going on outside."

I rotated my neck, lifted, and dropped my shoulders. *Get centered, business, money.*

Then I heard, "Hey c'mon, Sammy. Go get it! Fetch the stick."

I opened one eye. "I can't visualize two cents."

George arched a brow and lit up again. Smoke wreathed his head. "This is how you learn. Keep going until you get it."

Going through my relaxation routine again, this time I did it from head to toe. More deep breathing. Slowly, my mind began forming a picture. The wall calendar in my office came into focus. Afraid I would disturb the image, I remained perfectly still. The vision got clearer and I saw events and cities written on the calendar. The phone rang. *Hello. Yes, I'm available on that date.* Then, everything went blank. Opening my eyes, I was back sitting on the bench near Fanny Bridge. I actually felt a glimmer of hope.

George smiled. "When you stop resisting and engage your desires, you will see your dreams come true."

I clapped my hands, jumped up and down, and punched my fists in the air. "I can't believe it, I actually saw it!" I said with my voice rising. I stopped and looked at George. Then my impatience kicked in again. "But how long before it happens, Mr. Mentor?"

George shook his head. "First you visualize, then you follow through to make it reality. How long it takes depends on you and how dedicated you are. These levels of awareness require your time and attention."

I stared at him. "Does visualization work for everything?"

"Sure, and everyone," he replied.

"I'd like to hire someone for my office who complements my personality. A woman. Someone I can brainstorm with, who can help me take my business to the next level. After that last fiasco, when my marketing director stole from me, I need someone I can trust."

George agreed, tapping his pipe on the bench and stomping on the ashes as they fell to the ground. "Do the inner work and visualize that she's already working in your office. Maybe someone you know is going to introduce you to your new office partner."

I tossed George a dubious look. "When?"

"When you clearly state to the Universe what it is you want and need, that's when you draw it to you. Visualize every day."

"George, I hate to sound negative, but the economy is up and down. So how can I make a plan?"

"The outside world is always there to challenge you. It's your inner faith and determination that creates success. The man upstairs helps you when you help yourself. You've done it before, selling magazines, plants, pictures, motor homes, and even pots and pans door-to-door."

"But, George ..."

"Nope, don't go there," he said, shaking his head. "Don't focus on what you don't have. Let's focus on what you need now. I know you want to focus on a handsome man and a daughter, but right now you're going to visualize abundance and money in the bank."

George leaned back on the bench with a sigh. "All right, Partner, what is level three about?"

"I learned to tap my inner resources and visualize what I want."

George swept his hand upward in a large arc. "You got it."

Turning my life around wasn't going to be easy, but the future would be mine to claim. George had given me a good start, but I required support to keep going. Yearning for yet more guidance, I wondered if the fourth level would hold some magical power to help me with perseverance. "What's next, Mr. Spiritual Man?"

"A good question and I've got the answer," George said with a twinkle in his eye. "Let's do a homework assignment."

"Homework?"

"I promise no test. Close your eyes and visualize where you think the ideal location is in this mountain town to learn about the next level."

Closing my eyes I began. *Where ... where ... where,* my mind chanted. *Deep breath.* I could see fragments ... *trees ... restaurants ... no.*

I gave a sigh. "George, no clear picture is coming to mind."

"Close your eyes again and give it another shot."

Where ... where ... where ... lake ... beach ... rocks ... yes! That's it! "C'mon, George, we're going to Commons Beach. It's a local hangout. I'm going to challenge you to stone skipping."

George sprang to life. "That's an old Oklahoman pastime, so if you think you can beat me, you've got your work cut out for you."

> ***The more powerful your vision***
> ***the more it demands of you***

Chapter Six

Say It

What you say
is what you send out to the Universe
That's what you get back

"Look at it go!" Even I was impressed that my stone skipped four times. Hands on hips, heels dug into the sand, I said smugly, "See if you can beat that."

"Not bad," George commented. He was bent over, searching the shoreline for the perfect stone. "Hang on a minute and I'll give you a run for your money."

"Don't worry, broke as I am, you won't have to run far," I said while watching him move along the beach, past the tire swing and the spiral slide. I gazed at George's portly shape moving down the strand. Typically, the burden of other people's troubles weighed heavily on his mind and I rarely saw him so carefree.

A sage man, blessed with deep insight and wisdom, George spent a great deal of his time traveling the world and helping people by consulting on business affairs and counseling them on personal matters. Nowadays, he rarely took time for himself. He always remarked, "There are so many people to help and so little time."

Trudging back to where I waited, George gleamed, "Got some good ones. Watch closely." The rock skipped four times. He turned to me with a sparkle in his eyes. "How about that? We're tied."

"Good try, Mr. Wisdom Man, but you wait." I laughed wickedly, my eyes darting over the sand, hunting for the smoothest and flattest skippers. I came up with a champion. With victory in my heart, I focused with intensity and aimed my stone at the water.

To my disappointment, there were only three skips. George, on the other hand, had five skips and won the round. I tried again, and this time my stone skipped five times. Back in the running.

"Five, George," I said with resolve. "Five."

He grunted, took aim, and I counted. The little grey blur danced across the water seven times. My jaw dropped. "How did you do that? I never ..."

He chuckled. "Did I hear you say never? I'd say that kind of talk puts limits on your thinking. In fact, how you **say it** is the next level. Why don't we walk up the beach?"

I gazed at where he was pointing and saw a crowd of people taking in the sun, and children playing on the shore. With George huffing from the high altitude, we ambled along toward an outcropping of rocks. We passed an attentive woman with a toddler. The little girl threw her arms around the woman's leg saying, "Mommies, Mommies. I love you, Mommy. This is fun. Kisses." Then the bouncy child blew her mom a kiss while she ran ahead, singing.

George looked at them. "Isn't it wonderful to see the love of an innocent child?"

"Oh," I said, filled with envy as my eyes followed the woman and her little girl. "Will I ever have a child throw her arms around me and tell me she loves me? I want that more than anything in the world."

"Partner, you've asked that question dozens of times and my

answer is always the same. You have to believe it. When the time is right, and only when you're ready, then your daughter will arrive."

Watching the energetic girl dance in circles, I had no reason to doubt George, but I wondered if he understood how hard it was for me to be patient about becoming a mom. I was already in my mid-forties and running low on time and estrogen. I loved my fur baby, Sheba, but yearned for a daughter.

Farther on down the beach, we saw a small boy tossing stones into the water. A slim, dark-haired woman—his mother, I presumed—was standing nearby shouting words of encouragement. "Good job, Mark! That was a big splash. Now, stay nearby where I can see you."

Mark jumped up and down excitedly. "Mom, I love these rocks. I love 'em!" Simultaneously, George and I looked toward a huge mass of boulders rising from the water. Another young boy about Mark's size leapt from one boulder to the next, each time narrowly avoiding a fall into the lake. A tall woman came up from behind him and jerked his arm.

"What did I tell you, Tommy? I told you not to play here. You're going to fall and crack your head open or even worse, drown in the lake. Now, get down off those rocks this instant."

George touched a match to his pipe and was puffing rapidly to get it lit. My eyes were darting along the shoreline, searching for the perfect flat stone that would break his record of seven skips. "Look, there's snow on the mountain tops. We've already had one early snowfall and we skiers would love more."

My mentor peered across the lake and gave me his reassuring smile. "It's a spiritual sight when I see nature dressed in all her finery."

Suddenly, a splash and a woman's scream sliced through the air. A young boy was flapping his arms in the water. I grabbed George's arm, exclaiming, "Oh, no!" and started toward the boy, but George held up his hand, signaling me to wait. How could I wait? "For Pete's sake, the boy could be drowning!"

"Slow down, he'll be fine. Let's go over there."

Suddenly, a man pushed his way through the gathering crowd and dashed out across the rocks to reach the child. He jumped past the hysterical woman and leapt into the lake. My heart was pounding as I watched him grasp the boy by his sweatshirt and pull him from the water. From where we were standing, I could see that the child's mouth was open and gasping for air. Blood spurted from his forehead.

The man climbed out of the water with the child cradled in his arms, and scrambled over the rocks toward the beach. The shaking woman wept as she trailed closely behind.

I glanced at George and he nodded slowly as if to reassure me. Then I heard my inner voice say, *There are no accidents.*

When the trio reached the beach, the rescuer placed the boy gently on a blanket. Mark's mother appeared with a towel and handed it to the woman, who hugged the boy and began dabbing at his forehead.

I couldn't believe my ears when I heard her yelling again. "I told you not to play on the rocks. What's wrong with you? Why don't you listen?"

She dabbed at the boy's forehead again as his breathing returned to normal. "Can you walk to the car, Tommy? You must walk to the car. We have to go to the doctor to get your head stitched."

Tommy started crying, "No stitches! I'm scared I don't want—"

"No! We're going."

Then the man who rescued Tommy stepped forward. "I'll carry him to the car. It's going to be all right, son," he said reassuringly. "You'll be okay. You need to be checked out by a doctor."

George stood silently puffing on his pipe, his eyes glued to the scene before us. I saw him slowly shake his head again, and I could tell he wasn't pleased with Tommy's mother. Her behavior was scaring her son.

"Donna, you've just witnessed an example of level four, **say it**. It's all got to do with your words. Remember when we first saw Tommy and his mother? How she scolded him for climbing on the rocks, saying how he could fall and split his head open? What happened now was the result of the negative energy his mother put in motion. Yes, negative energy; the boy picked up on it and acted it out. Words are important. More powerful than you can imagine."

"Oh, I don't know. I don't believe that words alone could have caused that boy to fall in the water and get hurt. Think about it—didn't all our mothers yell, 'Don't run in the street—you'll get run over!'?"

"She should have acted out of love, but her fear and negativity created the circumstance that led to her son's injury. I will say it again," George said, "she attracted negative energy and the child reacted to what he was being told."

Tears brimmed in my eyes. "That's a lot to think about. You're telling me whatever I say could have big consequences?"

George shoved his hands into his pockets and gave me a reassuring nod. "I see you're getting a handle on level four."

"Can I change the subject and go back to the obsession that plagues me most?" I didn't wait for a reply but kept talking. "When I can get past all my issues, I truly want to be a good mom." I looked at George and could see that he was listening. "I've checked out a lot of adoption agencies, but most won't accept me because I'm single and in my forties. Most birth mothers want their child to be with a picture-perfect family: father, mother, dog, and picket fence."

"You can't blame them for that, Partner. But when the birth mother for your daughter appears, she'll recognize you as the best mom for her child."

His words warmed me. "There's an agency outside of San Francisco. The problem is, they want all the money up front, and I don't have it."

"You have to be aware of the words you're saying. Stop your fear. When you're in the fear pattern, she can't come to you. Let me ask you this: what are the top three things you want in life?"

"That I can answer. First, I have to master my emotions; second, I need financial stability; third, a daughter."

"Are you real clear on that being what you want?"

"Absolutely."

"You're sure?"

"Yes, I am sure. Yes, I am positive."

"Okay then. By the end of the day, I'm going to give you a gift to help you achieve those three goals."

"Really? You've never steered me wrong, Mr. Wisdom Man."

"Donna, I've enlightened you in the past about how you should talk to yourself. So let's go over **say it** again and have a little refresher course. Every morning before you get out of bed and every night before you go to sleep, I want you to say five positive statements to yourself. I call this 'self-talk,' and it works. It helps to say them out loud. Always start with the word 'I' and phrase it in the present tense. You might say something like, 'I am a loving person, I am happy, I have financial abundance, I am healthy, I am a great friend, I master my emotions, and I am a positive person.' Stay away from words like 'will' or 'try' because they are conditional and in the future."

I nodded, absorbing the words he was saying.

He continued, "You do not want to say something like, 'I will have the money to go on vacation in Hawaii.' Instead, state it like this: 'I have the money for my Hawaii vacation.' State your self-talk as if it's true, even if it isn't, because your goal is to create the energy to make it happen."

He took his hands from his pockets and narrowed his gaze on me.

I cleared my throat. "So, I say these things as if they are true, even if they are not?"

"You have to **say it** like you believe it. **Think it, feel it, visualize it,** and **say it** with meaning. Linking the levels together is what creates the power and attracts fulfillment." His brows knitted earnestly. "Repeat your positive self-talk throughout the day."

As if reading my mind, he said, "Believe me, it's powerful. You have to do the work every day and expect results."

George paused for one last look at the serene lake and the majestic mountains. Then we strolled leisurely back to the steps leading from the beach up to the street. Before climbing the steps, George hesitated. "Tell me what you're feeling, Donna."

After a few moments the exact words spontaneously burst from my mouth. "I am feeling better about myself."

With a self-satisfied nod and a huge smile, George confirmed, "Happy to hear that. Five positive statements each morning and night. Eliminate negative thoughts."

"Okay, I've got it; let's move on to level five. You know me, redheaded and Irish."

He laughed. "Hold your horses. Let's finish level four first. I want to sum up a few important points, and then we'll move on. Be clear about what you express to other people. Iffy words like 'someday,' 'maybe,' 'later,' 'if,' and 'I'll try,' should be tossed in your big lake here. Instead, speak positive statements like 'today,' 'definitely,' and 'now.'"

"Got it, Mr. Mentor."

He gave me one of his looks, then continued. "You might fool yourself into thinking level four is simple to master, but don't underestimate its importance. It's a driving force for getting you what you want."

Tahoe City was filling up with lunch-hour traffic. George and I stood on the cobblestones beneath the quick-moving clouds. He bent over the railing overlooking the beach and after a few seconds he said, "Partner, earlier you told me what you were feeling; now tell me what you've learned about level four."

"What did I learn? I learned the power of words. My wake-up call each morning is to say positive words. I should think before I speak, and communicate clearly to myself and others."

George chuckled. "Now you're ready for level five."

"Ready for a real eye-opener?" I asked, then laughed. "Our next location is picked out. My surprise is high in the sky, but we have to drive to get there. So, we'll get my car and then collect your luggage. Since my surprise is on the way to the airport, it'll work out perfectly." I loved every minute of this and played it to the hilt. "It's spectacular, breathtaking, nature at her finest, and it'll be a first for you." I giggled. "I know you've never done this, but I've done it hundreds of times."

George dug out his pipe and matches. He took a moment to light up and after several puffs of his aromatic cherry tobacco, he said with good humor, "So let's get a move on!"

What you think
what you say
is what you get

Chapter Seven

Do It

Every experience you undergo is a
chapter in your spiritual growth

We stood watching the slow-moving tram descending down the mountain, dangling from cable that looked so fragile a spider might have spun it. George was puffing like crazy on his pipe, eyes riveted on the tourist-filled tram careening in the wind.

He turned to me. "You have to be totally batty. You expect me to board that metal deathtrap and get hauled up over those jagged cliffs to the top of Squaw Valley?"

I was laughing so hard, I started to choke. After fielding a less-than-humorous look from George, I cleared my throat. "This really is a first. I don't recall ever hearing you say you were afraid of anything. I believe nothing could shake your faith. And by the way, when I ski I ride the tram to the top all the time."

"Well, Partner, I'm happy as a lark that you can do that." He pointed the stem of his pipe upward. "As for me, I'm not exactly crazy about heights. Been that way all my life."

"C'mon," I pressed, "the ticket booth is right over there at the entrance to the cable car building. You'll love the scenery. It's breathtaking."

George looked skeptical about my idea.

"You haven't lived until you've seen one of the most fabulous views in the world. George! Are you listening, or glaring at the tram?"

"I'm sure it's breathtaking all right," he conceded, "but I'd like to keep my feet on the ground as long as possible."

I ignored his comment and kept up my yammering. "Besides seeing all the natural wonders, you'll see people swimming, and even ice skating. It's spectacular."

"Partner, you're not selling me a vacation. This is my life we're talking about."

"Precisely," I agreed, and marched toward the turnstiles. George grudgingly trudged behind me. *So far so good*, I thought. "Hurry, let's get our tickets. They're loading the tram."

George raised his eyes to the heavens. "Where do they sell the parachutes?"

I giggled. "Not to worry. We won't need those until it's time to come down." He gave me another nervous look. "Only kidding."

Just seconds before the tram operator closed the doors, George bought our tickets, and we were the last to board. He was gripping the metal hand rails with both hands even before the tram began its steep climb. The car creaked and swayed as we gained momentum. After a few minutes, I glanced over at him as he stared tight-lipped out the window at the diminishing landscape below. When he closed his eyes, I figured he was asking God for help. He actually was being a brave sport, but I had to say something to calm his anxiety.

I reached out and patted his arm. "Squaw Valley is the ideal spot for our talk about how level five is special. Being on this mountain takes me closer to God, away from all the hubbub and commotion. That's why I wanted to bring you here."

Stealing a nervous peek at the disappearing landscape, he said, "Yup. Closer to God. That's where we're headed all right, nearer to God."

"Don't look down, George. If you look straight ahead, it's out of this world. C'mon, take a little teensy weensy peek," I urged, as he grunted in disbelief.

George's eyes fluttered open and grew wide behind his glasses. "Oh! It is a sight. Absolutely magnificent." He took a deep breath. "It would be even more impressive if I wasn't hyperventilating."

As we neared a jagged rock formation, a high support tower maneuvered the tram to bypass it, causing the car to sway back and forth. George and several other passengers gasped. "Don't worry," I stated confidently, "I've done this hundreds of times and I'm still here. A little bit longer and we're there."

The doors slid open at the summit, and George leapt out. With as much dignity as he could muster, and relief hitched to every one of his strides, he hurried along the covered walkway to the main building and collapsed on the nearest bench. Heaving a huge sigh, he exclaimed, "I love having the earth beneath my feet."

"You did great, Mr. Miracle Man. Speaking of feet, get back on them. There's something I must show you."

George muttered a comment about no mercy as I led him to the scenic lookout. A brilliant sun shone through the branches of towering green giants as we gazed out at the sweeping landscape and the sparkling waters of majestic Lake Tahoe. Glancing upward at an enormous outcropping of rocks reaching for the sky, I saw snow as white as whipped cream crowning the mountain tops. In a couple of months, the entire area would be blanketed in white. My heart swelled to near bursting at the sight of this splendid fairyland. Turning to George and glimpsing the delight in his eyes, I noticed his earlier tension had vanished.

"This is glorious—a whale of a view. Nature and the man upstairs joined together. It was worth risking life and limb to get here," he said, followed with an inevitable chuckle. "Well, almost."

"Did I choose the right site to learn the last level?"

He stared at the lush scenery below, then turned and scanned the ominous mountain tops. "It's perfect. You couldn't have done better, Partner. When we have fears to confront, we humans tend to remove ourselves from the situations that offer us the most growth potential. The tram ride was a fitting reminder for me."

George had always been a profound person—large, strong, and wise, a spiritual being with a reverence for life, surrounded by an aura of divinity and calm. Today I witnessed his human side.

Fumbling for words, I confessed, "You know, I've certainly had my share of fears in my lifetime. Mostly I feared that I wasn't good enough—not slim enough, not adequate for the men I chose, and then there's my career—not smart enough. Now when I think back, I realize the real problem was that I didn't like myself much. After the plane crash I underwent a productive period of growth. And you, Mr. Wise Sage, enlightened me with your transcendent wisdom by helping me overcome the fearful limitations I'd put upon myself."

"Ah." George nodded. "I've learned one thing for certain in my years of helping people. When you're sick and tired of being sick and tired, you'll change. You can never avoid problems—not the big ones or the little ones. If you use the levels you learned today—**think it**, **feel it**, **visualize it**, and **say it**—then results happen when you use the final level: **do it.**"

"**Do it,** that's the final level?"

"It sure is, Partner."

"George, I think I have an idea of what you're talking about. We're standing on a great example of the last level. The 1960 Olympics were held right here in Squaw Valley. Athletes trained and prepared, but the real results happened during the competition."

I arced an arm out to emphasize the expansive setting. "We're only seeing the view from one side of the mountain. If you take a chair lift to the other side, you see Shirley Lake and an area called Granite Chief." Then I pointed to a tall, isolated peak. "Up there is Siberia. Can you guess why it has that name?"

George pulled out his tobacco pouch and filled his pipe while staring up at Siberia. "Well, it looks mighty unfriendly and cold to me."

"Right on."

He lit up, drew on his pipe, and the scent of cherries permeated the air as he tossed me an uneasy look. "You're not thinking about talking me into going up there, are you?"

Laughing uncontrollably, I said, "I wouldn't dare, though I do love skiing there. Sometimes when my brain gets muddled, going up to Siberia has a cleansing effect. I sure hope my daughter likes this mountain as much as I do."

My mentor didn't comment, but had a faraway look in his eyes and slowly nodded. Finally he said, "This is a healing place for you."

"Healing place ... sure, I always feel good up here," I quickly stated.

Still not looking at me he softly said, "Yes, this is a healing place for you."

"What do you mean?" I stared at him for what seemed like eternity. Suspecting George wasn't going to say anything else, I continued, "Let's get a move on. There's more to see."

We strolled past the ice-skating rink, the oversized heated pool surrounded with granite boulders, and into a trendy bar. George ambled over to an empty table, sat down, and motioned for me to pull up a chair. For a man who was scared out of his socks an hour ago, he seemed to be relaxed and having a good time.

"Donna, the next level is important. It is **do it**. This is about uniting all the levels and moving forward. When you think about building something, you first visualize how it's going to look when it's finished, right?"

"Sure." I wondered where he was going with this. Was I going to get another Georgeism?

"You draw the blueprint and lay a foundation to construct the building. Personally and professionally create what you want in your mind, then do the work with purpose and passion."

He shook his head. "Don't sweat the small stuff. Sort out what's important to you and go after it. Taking some action is better than none at all. Whatever you're thinking about doing, whether changing your job or planning a family, you have to feel it's right all the way down to your toes. Do you feel it in your gut? Does your head say it's okay?"

I listened, captivated.

"Three things can happen," George continued. "You don't perceive an answer, you feel unsettled and uncomfortable, or you're calm. The secret is to meditate and listen for the answer. Then let your intuition guide you. Think of your inner soul as a messenger who comes beating his wings at your door with a special gift. If you don't open the door and greet the messenger, you don't get the gift. It takes discipline, but I have some tricks up my sleeve to help you get going." George studied me through narrowed eyes. "Let me ask you a question. Do you still like professional speaking?"

"Of course I do. I love speaking."

"Is there anything you don't like about your work?"

"Yes."

"Care to share that with me?"

"I don't like making cold calls. I don't like getting rejected."

"Uh-huh, but you have to show up at your desk and make those calls to get work, don't you? There's always something we don't like about every job, but it has to be done."

I shrugged. "It's going to take some kind of miracle to turn me around."

"I happen to have a miracle. I'm going to show you how to rebuild your life."

"Really?"

"Yes, but before we go any further, I feel hunger pangs coming on. I need a plateful of energy before I can make you a believer."

George gave me one of his devilish smiles. "You know the rules. Feed me first. Can I get a burger or a sandwich?"

"Lucky for you, there's plenty of food up here. It got here the same way you did, on the tram."

We were headed toward the restaurant when our attention turned to a group of people laughing and cheering. Stopping in his tracks, George observed a man plunging into the yawning abyss on the end of a bungee cord. With pursed lips he said, "It has to be something in the California water making people this crazy. Is there a name for that death-defying pastime?"

I giggled. "It's called bungee jumping. Want to give it a try?"

"Not in this lifetime. I've heard about crazy people flying by their ankles, but I've never seen it up close and personal. Though it's not as bad as I thought; it's worse!"

"You know Californians—they like extreme sports."

The aroma in the rustic restaurant was enticing as we entered. George ordered ham and cheese on sourdough, with a mug of his beloved black coffee, and I opted for a veggie burger on wheat with a hot chocolate. The only thing on my mind was talking. Smiling contentedly, he sat back in his chair, always happy when the scent of food was nearby.

"Explain to me why some people succeed and others don't," I demanded.

"Don't you ever ask easy questions?" George looked thoughtful, and inched forward in his chair. "I'll do my best to simplify it. The world is full of love and has its share of hate. There are talkers and doers, the powerless and the powerful, those who seek themselves and those who are themselves. People take different paths and play many roles. Success is more of a perception than anything else. Everyone has their own idea of what success is. It all depends on what you want and the choices you make. What were your fears about being successful?"

At first his question caught me off guard. "Hmm. One, I couldn't make it without a man. Two, I wasn't smart enough to run my own business."

George sipped his newly warmed coffee and set the mug back on the table. "Your fears became reality."

"They sure did. I allowed other people to steal my power: the boyfriend I foolishly put on the title to my house, and the marketing director who stole from me."

He reached over and patted my hand. "Having learned those painful lessons, and opening yourself to change, you embarked on a spiritual transformation I call *the knowing*."

"Please explain *the knowing* again. I recall you saying that I needed to develop my intuition first."

George raised his eyebrows and said, "We all have five basic senses: sound, sight, smell, taste, and touch. In a nutshell, *the knowing* is the ability to detect knowledge beyond the capability of those basic senses. Your intuition reveals the answer to you. Without a question of a doubt, you know it is right. That's *the knowing*. The most important aspect is to trust it and take action right away."

Reaching underneath his sweatshirt, he removed several envelopes and laid them on the table. Each envelope was numbered, 1 through 5. "What you see here are 30 days of awareness to help develop your intuition. They are a collection of thoughts, self-talks, and affirmations that will nurture your development."

I reached out a hand, but George slapped it. "Uh-uh. Can't open them up until after I'm gone; otherwise, I'll be here for the whole week answering your questions. This is my present to you. I call it the gift of intuition. I won't always be here, and you'll need strength to carry on."

A part of me protested and a shiver dashed up my spine. "George, don't say that. You'll always be here."

"Yes, but not as you know me today. You won't be able to pick up the phone and call me, but I'll be around when you need me. The soul never dies and I'll hear your words. We'll communicate differently, but you must first master the skill of intuition so you'll hear my message come through. It's getting late, and I'd like to give you some suggestions on working with the gift of intuition. Focus each day on the affirmation and implement it into your daily life. Call me at the end of each week and we'll talk."

"That's it?"

"The knowledge you seek will be revealed by reading the gift of intuition."

For a moment, time stood still as if to capture the significance of this day. I felt compelled to ask, "George, are you my angel?"

"Someday you'll know. Right now it's time to head for the airport." He chuckled. "Is going down the mountain easier than coming up?"

I glanced at the bundle of envelopes. "Yes," I teased, "you can fly down."

 Journal
Do It

*If you don't open the door
and greet the messenger
you don't get the gift*

George came to visit me today, and what a day to remember. I had been bugging him for years to teach me about intuition. And he had to pick today, a day I felt like a truck had run over me. He has this mystical quality; he knew exactly when to show up. I'll admit I was going a little haywire, so he arrived with a mission to change all that. I wonder, Do other people have these kinds of self-defeating thoughts blasting through their mind?

I am looking at these envelopes and I want to open them now, but George insisted I have to wait until morning. I wonder if morning is 12:01 AM or first light? I'll wait. Job one: lock these levels in my mind.

- **Level One - Think It**
- **Level Two - Feel It**
- **Level Three - Visualize It**
- **Level Four - Say It**
- **Level Five - Do It**

Sure sounds simple enough, like: "drink eight glasses of water a day," "exercise on a regular basis," and "cut out sugars." Still working on those challenges. Why do I have the feeling George's gift of intuition sounds easy, but living it will be another story? I'll have to wait and see what unfolds.

Thank you, God. Thank you, George. I ask whatever messages are in these envelopes to enlighten my soul.

I accept change
I welcome it
with an open heart

Part II

The Gift of Intuition

Chapter Eight
Is Your Attitude Showing?

Believing is the first step
toward making change happen

Awakening with a yawn, I sat up in bed and switched on the light. Even though it was still dark, I couldn't wait any longer to start Day 1 of George's gift of intuition. The first envelope was propped up on my nightstand. Eager as a presenter at the Oscars, I tore open the envelope and unfolded a sheet of bond paper marked with my name and the words *Read First* in George's handwriting.

Dear Donna,

Within these five envelopes are thirty affirmations to enable the gift of intuition. Whatever you want to call them, affirmations or empowering thoughts, it's important to believe in their power. Believing is the first step toward making change happen. As the days go by while you focus on the messages, you'll sense a shift, as your inner values start directing your outer actions. As you progress, transformations will take place, and you'll discover the answers to many of the questions you have asked me.

*The gift of intuition is available to anyone. Consider this a new beginning on a higher path to self-knowledge and spiritual well-being. Every day, you'll remove the negativity and doubt in your life and live the levels of **think it, feel it, visualize it, say it,** and **do it.** It's imperative that you integrate these levels so they become a natural part of your life. This will allow your intuition to manifest. But, if you harbor anger at yourself or someone else, it blocks you and your intuition will be tainted by your emotional turmoil.*

These affirmations are life-changing, empowering thoughts that will fill you with awareness. Read one affirmation each day, and focus on your daily thoughts. But I know you, and I have the feeling you will read a week's worth when you open the envelope. You need to remember that each one builds on the affirmation of the day before, so you can learn to live these qualities in your everyday routine. Be open to all possibilities. As you do this, you will attract results. These qualities will heighten your intuition, and you will be guided to make positive decisions. I believe in you. I look forward to your call at the end of each week.

George

I pulled out seven pieces of paper. As I flipped through them, each one was titled with a day number, an insight, and ended with an affirmation. I held them tightly in my hand and flipped through them like a speed reader. Next, I ran down the hall, turned on the overhead light, and spread them out on my kitchen counter in numerical order, then read each one slowly, trying to absorb all the knowledge on the papers. I noticed some of the papers seem to be more worn than others. My hope was that the information would transmit instantly to my brain.

Day 1

Attitude

You determine the outcome of each day when you wake up and your feet hit the floor. You decide whether it will be an intolerable day or a successful one, because 87% of success is attitude and 13% is skill.

Neither fame, fortune, nor beauty entitles you to a bad attitude. Improving your attitude is the first step toward changing your life. When your attitude centers on optimism, integrity, and managing your state, it empowers you.

Your attitude does NOT depend on the actions or behavior of other people. It's one thing that you totally create.

AFFIRMATION: I manage my attitude to create positive results.

Day 2

Confidence

Confidence is earned from learning the lessons you experience. It helps to define your actual purpose and it is supported by your values. It's the building block to success and the cement that keeps you from giving up. Like life, your confidence can experience highs and lows. Confidence is the belief in your own abilities to succeed. Only you can manage your confidence and no one has the right to take it away from you.

Listen to the voice inside you, trust your intuition and your feelings, and then take action. Self-confidence is an essential trait, and a worthy quality to encourage in others.

AFFIRMATION: I am balanced, focused, and confident.

After I finished reading Day 2, I realized this was going to be a process, so I turned on the stove and brewed a cup of tea. Curled in a chair, mug in hand, I re-read Day 2 again and realized that confidence was definitely lacking in my life. I laid the page down and continued on through Day 7.

Day 3
Values

Values are your beliefs. They determine the way you think, and the choices you make. They are not materialistic things like new cars, jewelry, vacations, or designer labels. The values you choose should honor and inspire your spirit. Love, security, health, and family are important values to many people. You can also focus on spiritual enlightenment.

There is no correct and complete list of values. They are not common interests, like movies and tennis, but beliefs such as work, honesty, and kindness that bind people together. We set our standards by first establishing our values. Determine your top five values, then work to not compromise them, and they will guide you to fulfillment.

AFFIRMATION: I live my values.

Day 4
Emotions

Emotions are the way we express our feelings. They communicate our happiness, pain, anger, and love. They are as necessary to your well-being as breathing.

Emotions can frequently fluctuate up and down. The energy you provide them often determines your reaction in certain situations. Negative emotions like fear, anger, and depression create unhealthy results and impair progress. Taking time out to understand the true reason behind emotional upset provides an opportunity to see the larger picture, and reach a more productive conclusion.

Mastering emotions like love, compassion, and patience gives you personal power. Before you fly off the handle, take ten seconds to consider the situation. Good communication, creativity, and wholesome relationships are important to your emotional well-being.

AFFIRMATION: I master my emotions.

Day 5

Responsibility

Responsibility means being accountable, making clear and rational decisions, and taking meaningful action. Irresponsibility manifests when people procrastinate and blame others for their misfortunes and mistakes. Avoid being a finger-pointer.

When you make a mistake own up to it; take immediate steps to amend it. Learning from your mistakes helps you to make better choices and claim responsibility.

Rather than complain, shoulder your obligations. Acknowledge that you are responsible for your behavior. Love and nurture your relationships and honor your commitments to yourself and others. Embracing your responsibility helps you manifest your dreams and expands your personal and professional power.

AFFIRMATION: I am responsible for my thoughts and actions.

I almost spilled my hot tea on myself while reading this one again, knowing sometimes I didn't want to claim responsibility for my problems because blaming someone else was easier.

Day 6

Integrity

Integrity helps define character, credibility, and honor. When faced with a dilemma, it is tempting to seek a quick and easy answer. Instead, you must ask yourself if there is a moral message in your predicament.

Everyone faces the consequences of their actions sooner or later. Whatever the situation, did you give it your full attention? Were you completely honest? Did you blame someone else? Or were you forthright in all your affairs, claiming responsibility for each and every action?

Being of sound moral principle is not always easy and often requires more effort than we believe we can give. Let integrity guide your conscience and design your code of ethics.

AFFIRMATION: I have integrity in all situations.

Day 7

Meditation

Meditation is a calm state of relaxation that creates spiritual and physical well-being. Begin by meditating three times a week for ten or fifteen minutes at a time. Once the process becomes more natural, you will want to meditate more often to help release stress and restore energy.

To begin, turn off all the distractions in your space and clear your mind. Find a comfortable chair, light a scented candle, and play soft music or a guided meditation CD. Close your eyes, breathe deeply, relax your body, and invite serenity to settle over you.

Meditation is a quiet reflection to help you reach within and bring harmony and healing into your life. Meditation promotes intuition and attracts the knowledge to help you make better decisions. Meditate often because it heightens your total awareness and spiritual enlightenment.

AFFIRMATION: I meditate for inner peace and wisdom.

I placed the pages by my bed and each morning of the week I read one, contemplated it, and then repeated the affirmation throughout my day.

I did it! I completed the seven days of the gift of intuition. I couldn't wait to call George. First, I rehearsed what I would say, then, I dialed his number. Disappointment was what I felt when I was told he was in a meeting that would last another hour. An hour was a long time when the only thing occupying my mind was talking to my mentor.

Pacing the floor I opened the fridge. Cheese, salad, leftover pasta—nothing looked good, so I closed the fridge and checked the clock. Thirty seconds later I checked my watch. It's funny how things have a weird way of slowing down when you are killing time. I went into the living room, did some stretches followed by jumping jacks. Finally, an hour had passed; I dialed, mumbling to myself, "Come on George. Be there. Mr. Wise Man. Talk to me."

"Well, Partner," he said with a chuckle, "I've been expecting your call. Tell me, how are you doing with the gift of intuition?"

"Boy, were my emotions controlling me instead of me controlling my emotions," I stated excitedly. "I can't believe—"

"Whoa there, Partner. Slow down, sit down, and calm down."

I flopped on the sofa.

"Are you sitting down?"

"Yes, sir. Yes I am."

"Okay. Now tell me again, slower please. How's your state of mind?"

"I can honestly say it's better. I did what you asked and completed the entire seven days. Okay George, I sneaked a peek ... um, I looked at all seven days at once. You know me—no patience; I'll work on it in this lifetime, just not today. I laid the papers out on my kitchen counter."

I paused for a second to gather my thoughts. Then I continued, "Well, I did integrate all the insights into the week. Now I have so much stuff in my head, it's backed up like a traffic jam. I started with attitude, then confidence, values—that was interesting—then emotions ... need I say more? But George," I grumbled, "I still don't have any money."

"Uh-huh. Well, that'll come. Do you have questions about any of the affirmations? Some more challenging than others?"

I snickered. "Me, not have any questions? That's like the Pacific not having any water. I thought after the plane crash the worst was over and each day would be better than the last. What I'm realizing now is that it just doesn't happen. If I want to be more than I am today, I have to do the work. Some of the affirmations really got me thinking."

I heard George puffing on his pipe at the other end of the line. "Sounds like the affirmations triggered some solid thinking."

"Oh, yes, let's talk about Day 4: responsibility. I wasn't claiming mine. I was blaming others for my problems—clients not calling me and my ex-boyfriend screw-up. I need to claim responsibility in my career and in my love life. I can alter that by doing what I learned on Day 7, the meditation stuff. But you know me—I can turn into a jumping bean at times. Meditation and I usually go together like oil and water, but I've placed a candle and a guided meditation CD in a quiet spot, and I'm setting aside fifteen minutes each afternoon. I used to meditate, George, and for some reason I got busy and stopped. Now I'm back on track. I understand about clearing the clutter from my mind and getting calm, but my difficulty is being still long enough to actually listen to the answer."

"Hmm," George agreed. "I never said it was easy, but you learned a lot this week. Do you notice any change in your energy?"

I thought about what he asked, and then said, "I don't understand."

"Did you have more energy? Did you get out of bed early each morning?"

"I'm calmer than when you last saw me."

"I'm glad I extended my time in Tahoe. I'd say your progress is about on target."

I could almost smell his cherry smoke coming across the line. "You know, I'm so blessed to have you in my life. How do people hold their lives together without a George?"

"Partner, there's always someone to talk to. It could be a parent, a teacher, an aunt or uncle, a neighbor, or a friend. Never forget, if a person wants to talk, the man upstairs is always ready to listen as well. The average person usually doesn't want all the answers in one day. Unlike you, they take an occasional breather. But your persistent side wants firsthand answers now. Sometimes I think it would be easier to win a dog sled race with a team of Chihuahuas than deal with your want-it-now attitude."

That got me chuckling. "Seriously, those affirmations sound simple, but have huge meaning."

"Time for my next meeting, Partner. Are you ready to open envelope number two? Don't forget to wait until morning."

"All right, I won't cheat."

"There's some pretty valuable stuff coming up. I think ... well ... I'm even going to give you a hint."

"What is it? Out with it."

"Okay. It begins with the letter B."

I let loose an exasperated groan. "Big deal. C'mon, you can do better than that, Mr. Wise Man."

"It's something you want. You want it on the inside and you want it on the outside. But, you have to have one to have the other."

Thinking as a woman, I laughed and said, "Sounds like a pair of shoes."

George ignored my comment.

"Oh, I've got it! B, for baby! I want her more than anything in the world. I want that on the inside and the outside."

"Not exactly what I was thinking. Keep living the affirmations. Open the envelope tomorrow and you'll be surprised. Call me in a week."

Journal
Is Your Attitude Showing?

The gift of intuition
is more valuable than gold

Funny how easily I can get off track. When I saw my ex-boyfriend with his new wife, I felt devastated and overcome with negativity.

George, good old George, so simple yet so complex, made me stop in my tracks and look at my life differently. Sometimes I'm scared to change and I know I give him a hard time because of my fear. Please accept my apology.

From the gift of intuition I understand how crucial it is to keep my attitude positive ALL THE TIME! Easier said than done. Confidence; I do bounce up and down from moments of great creativity to thoughts of suicide. So that brings me to Day 3: values, the beliefs I live my life by. The best way to develop my intuition is by meditation, and the side benefit is it aligns my emotions to be more calm.

George, what a worthy present you have given me. The gift of intuition is more valuable than gold. I am blessed that you believe in me even when I'm having a pity party. My mission is to live these affirmations so I can develop my intuition. I will repeat them out loud before I fall asleep.

Attitude
Confidence
Values
Emotions
Responsibility
Integrity
Meditation

Chapter Nine
Can't Live Without It

When you awaken each morning
you can choose to set your mood for the day

I glanced at the clock. 11:47 AM already? Where had the morning gone? Between client phone calls and e-mails I hadn't had time to open my envelope. Break time. Skipping every other step from my office to my kitchen, the only thing on my mind was tearing open the envelope. As I rushed into the kitchen my fluffy white, blue-eyed cat Sheba cranked up her motor and started weaving in and out of my legs, reminding me that she was hungry. She demanded all my attention. "Queen Sheba, I'm feeding you as fast as I can."

Reaching for the envelope sitting on the kitchen table, my inner voice screamed, *STOP!* I was too anxious; I was rushing like a crazy woman. I was in no frame of mind to comprehend what this small but mighty assignment meant. I was overeager to see what was in the envelope. Nothing could stop me. Sheba leaped up on the kitchen table and landed right on top of the envelope. Startled at first, I then chuckled. I tousled Sheba's head and said, "Have you been talking to George? Did he tell you I have to be centered when I read my insights?" I backed up toward the stove. "I'm calming down; I'm making a cup of tea."

Sipping from my favorite mug, I peered out the kitchen window. The golden-orange colors of fall were beckoning me to come outside and bask in their beauty. It was a crisp, sunny early afternoon and I knew that in only a few months, a layer of snow would cover the entire back yard.

I scooped up the envelope, and, taking my tea outside to the backyard, Sheba followed me and then perched herself on a rock. Surrounded by crimson holly berries, deep purple dogwood, and the rust-gold shimmer of maple leaves, it was easy to imagine myself without a care in the world. As I looked intently at the envelope, I suddenly understood the real reason behind George granting me the gift of intuition. He was helping a stubborn, confused soul become grounded.

Sheba snuggled close to me and rolled over to sun herself. It was as if she was saying, Now you're calm enough to open the next envelope. I put down my tea cup, ripped open the envelope marked "2," and started reading the next week's worth of affirmations.

Day 8

Health

Good health heightens your passion and enthusiasm for life. Like a cocoon that houses a beautiful butterfly, your body shelters your soul. If you abuse your body with a poor diet, addiction, or excessive stress, you injure your soul as well. Depression, anger, and even lack of self-esteem can result.

Focus on ways to nurture your health. Drink plenty of water to rid your body of toxins and aid digestion. Avoid eating junk food that can clog the pathways to vital organs. You want to stay heart-healthy. Remember what

Mom said about eating plenty of fresh fruits and vegetables? She was right. Your body needs a reliable supply of vitamins and minerals to keep your brain and organs in good working order to prevent disease.

Mark your calendar every year for your dental check-up and a doctor visit. Establish clear communication with your doctors so you are committed to a healthy regimen. You're worth it.

AFFIRMATION: I am healthy in body, mind, and spirit.

After glancing at all the affirmations that were in this envelope, I strolled back into the kitchen, spread out my new assignments, and stood over them. I read them one at a time, praying they somehow were being absorbed throughout my entire body. After reading them twice I held Day 8 in my hand and paced around the house, reading it again and again out loud.

Day 9

Exercise

The more you exercise, the stronger and more confident you'll feel. Choose an activity that suits your needs and temperament. Even if you have a back problem, a brisk walk or a refreshing swim can be an excellent and safe aerobic exercise. Commit to your exercise on a regular basis. No excuses. Just do it! It isn't necessary to become a long-distance runner or seek the perfect body.

If you lack motivation, work out with a friend who can boost your involvement and solidify your sense of commitment. Exercise relieves stress and keeps you focused. It boosts your quality of life and longevity. Consider aerobics, hiking, biking, weightlifting, swimming, golf, or yoga. Get your body moving, do something wonderful for yourself, and keep healthy. It's never too late to start an exercise program. Today is the day.

AFFIRMATION: I commit to exercise each week.

Day 10
Balance

Having balance in your personal and professional life brings you stability and satisfaction. Balance is essential to create inner harmony and symmetry with the people around you.

For most people, there are eight important facets to life: family, social, physical, education, professional, financial, attitude, and spiritual. The challenge is to maintain healthy proportions in each area.

Like dominoes, if you are out of balance in one or more areas, there will be a chain reaction affecting your entire well-being. For example, if you do not engage in regular physical exercise, it will impact your attitude at work because you'll lack energy and won't have an outlet to burn off your stress.

When you're out of balance, immediately take measures to correct the imbalance by putting more time and energy into those areas being neglected. Staying positive and being aware are the first steps in maintaining a healthy balance.

AFFIRMATION: I create balance in my life.

I stood in front of the paper again and studied what I had read. *Balance. Not a quality that I am really familiar with. Could it be that being out of balance makes me a little crazy? This affirmation will take some time for me to process. How can I trust my intuition if I am always out of balance.* "Hmm, Mr. Mentor, you are wise. I can't trust my intuition if I am out of balance. Now I'm starting to understand your reasoning in building these affirmations upon each other.

Day 11
Relationships

The ability to communicate and interact with others is vital to establishing healthy relationships. As with your roles in life, your relationships will vary depending upon circumstances. For example, we connect with ourselves, God, family, friends, and even pets. There are many levels of relationships, some close and interactive, and others more impersonal.

Your goal is to instill harmony, cooperation, and real values into your relationships. Respect your differences, treat people as you wish to be treated, and avoid judgment. Above all, be honest with yourself and others. Let down your barriers, conquer fear, laugh, cry, love, and prosper. Form lasting bonds with those you care about.

AFFIRMATION: I have positive relationships.

Day 12
Humor

Laughter is a wonderful way to bring serenity to the soul. Seeing the humor in stressful situations helps you to laugh at yourself and lighten your mood. When circumstances don't go your way, relieve your frustration with humor.

Humor diminishes anger. Think about how you feel in a tense situation when someone cracks a joke at just the right time and the tension dissipates. It's fun to be around people who are upbeat and lighthearted. Science has proven that the more humor and laughter you enjoy in your life, the longer and healthier you'll live.

AFFIRMATION: I laugh easily and often.

Day 13

Inner Peace

When you awaken each morning you can choose to set your mood for the day. Sure, there will be situations that irritate you, but you can elect to not let them control your attitude and demeanor. Inner peace is a state of mind that you can develop through meditation, by calming your thoughts and connecting with your spirit.

Rid yourself of anger, judgment, and prejudice, for these negative thoughts destroy your potential for serenity. Inner peace is a virtue you can develop and nurture.

To create inner peace, take a few deep breaths, focus on what is really important, and wait for a calm feeling before speaking or acting. Replace negative thoughts with loving and affirming ones to help improve your peaceful attitude.

AFFIRMATION: I manifest inner peace.

Day 14

Spirituality

On a daily basis, trust your inner voice and your relationship with God to guide and enlighten you. Spirituality gives you awareness and fulfillment. If it is your wish to mature spiritually, seek ways to enhance your inner contentment. Your spirit also connects you with nature.

The definition of spirituality is that which relates to the human soul as opposed to material or physical things. Prayer is how you ask for help or guidance. Meditation is the way you listen for the answer. Owning spirituality is to exist at a higher level of awareness. You can help friends or neighbors in need, become active in your child's school, volunteer for a charity, or work in a local hospital. By combining worldly acts of kindness with spiritual energy, you acquire purpose and fulfillment.

AFFIRMATION: I am a spiritual being.

After these seven days of consistent practice, I had completed another week of empowering affirmations. I was definitely beginning to feel a change in myself. A round of applause! I made it through Day 14 and I was beginning to feel more optimistic. The big B had turned out to be balance; I would never have guessed that. I read that affirmation a half dozen more times. The goal was to allocate time and energy among eight areas of my life: family, social, physical, education, professional, financial, attitude, and spiritual. Who was I kidding? Let me see, which ones were out of balance? Oh, that's right—all of them.

I could hardly control my excitement as I dialed George's number. He wasn't in Oklahoma, so I phoned Denver and was given a number to call him in Dallas.

After dialing Dallas, I was informed that he had taken a quick trip to South America and would be returning that night. Frustrated, I left a message for him to call me first thing in the morning. This gave me more time to process the new ideas I had swimming around in my head. My big, overstuffed living room chair was calling my name to come and meditate. Then I would go to bed and sleep like a baby—at least that was my plan.

The ringing phone jarred me awake. I opened my eyes and squinted at the digital clock. Five-thirty, oh, that would be George. Bolting straight up, I snatched the phone and exclaimed, "Hello,

George."

"Hey, Partner, did I wake you?" He chuckled. "Can't catch any worms lying around in bed."

"Hey, I'm not Tweety Bird. I don't fly and I don't eat worms."

Another chortle. "Nice to know your humor woke up with you." A pause. "How is the gift of intuition coming along?"

Deciding to dodge the subject until I was fully awake I said, "Hey, you didn't tell me you were going to South America."

"Well, I had some people to help down there. So, what's up? I've got a heavy schedule, but I've set aside some time for you."

Reaching up, I turned on the light. "First of all, Mr. Early Bird, I'm curious. How did you put together the gift of intuition program? It sums up your Georgeisms, plus has loads more information."

I heard him take a second to flick a match and light his pipe. After a few puffs he said, "It's a collection of insights, with odds and ends from near and faraway places, from a whole array of people, created with a lot of help from the man upstairs."

After some pipe puffing, George continued, "I'm curious: how did you do on Day eight, health?"

I swallowed hard. "Do I have to tell you?"

"Only if you want to improve yourself."

"I abused my body by being bulimic for years during my Hollywood stint. You know, a self-defeating feeding frenzy: high on health food one week, then diving into bags of cookies the next. As if that wasn't bad enough, I foolishly thought my self-confidence would improve through destructive dieting."

"What were you not dealing with emotionally that made you sabotage your health?" George countered.

"I ... I don't know what you mean."

"Yes, you do. Answer my question."

I sighed heavily, then blurted out, "I thought I wasn't good enough."

"Well well, that old demon, lack of self-esteem, had shown up on your doorstep. Health and hope are connected. Let's move on to Day nine."

"Health and hope are connected. Let's move on, to Day 9."

I thought for a moment. *Exercise.* "There's months when I'm spectacular—hiking, skiing, and going to the gym. Then there are months when I'm an absolute no-show. I find ways to dodge working out, and sit around like a lump with no energy."

"Partner, it's the consistency of doing exercise on a regular basis that keeps you healthy. I know how you love sports and have exercised on and off throughout your life. You've got to create consistency, not feast or famine, as you did with your diet, and make it a priority."

"Aren't you the pot calling the kettle black? You're a far cry from being an exercise enthusiast," I reminded him.

"That jumping around stuff is not my piece of cake, but I like to walk and heaven knows I need to do more of it."

"Yes, you do. I want to make sure you're around for a long time to come."

Ignoring my comment, George asked, "So how did you do on the big B?"

"You have no idea how I puzzled over what the big B might be. I thought, the Big Apple, big bucks, and baby bassinet. I wasn't even close. Balance!"

George chuckled as I continued, "The good news is, I need to work plenty on all eight areas."

"Don't be so hard on yourself. You've got your work cut out for you, but I know you can do it. Let's move on to the next one."

"So you mean the R word, relationships? Heck, you've heard it all and you understand I need a major overhaul in this area. Too many men, or no decent man. He loves me, he loves me not. Can't live with him, can't live without him. So I do not have a handle on this category."

He snickered. "At least you haven't lost your sense of humor."

"That's because when it comes to humor, I have a five-star rating. Through all my trials and tribulations, humor has been my constant companion. Maybe I need more humor in my relationships, since they are so tough for me to maintain. Although, I do have an outstanding one with my cat, and some of my friends as well. Will I ever have a loving relationship with a man?"

"Before that can happen, you need to have a loving relationship with yourself." He continued talking with enthusiasm. "Start by creating an aura of inner peace."

"Yes, Day thirteen was inner peace."

"Donna, the outside world always wants more from you. There is a place of rest within yourself—a quiet place, which, when mastered creates attraction on its own. You can raise your level of awareness and revitalize yourself through meditation. Your main task boils down to working on balance," George counseled. "I'll have to go soon. Are you ready to open the next envelope?"

"Sure. Give me a hint of what to expect. A good hint so I know what you are talking about."

"Hmm." He paused to think. "You'll be working on A creates A."

"A creates A," I repeated. "Alignment creates abundance? Acceptance creates ambiance? Come on, Mr. Sage Man, tell me."

"Time for me to go. Talk to you next week."

That's so like him, I thought. He would give me information, but not answers. It was my job to figure things out for myself. I placed the receiver back in the cradle and noticed my journal sitting open on the nightstand. I decided to read it.

Journal
Can't Live Without It

George had been so kind in giving me a hint, which was the big B. I was sure it meant BABY, and that I would have my imaginary little daughter in my arms in no time. As it turned out I wasn't even close; he meant balance. Now, when I think about it, that makes much more sense. After all, who respects the kind of person who says, "Puppy, puppy, puppy, I must have that dog," when she hasn't the physical or emotional means to care for it? Stability will be important in my life if I'm ever going to raise a daughter. Inner peace and spirituality would be wonderful traits to pass on to a child. And please, Lord, let her NOT be blessed with my dramatic flair.

I commit to being healthy, and that means exercising and eating right. I AM ON IT! A healthy program is on my agenda. God, grant me the strength to continue on this positive path.

Health
Exercise
Balance
Relationships
Humor
Inner Peace
Spirituality

Chapter Ten

Act and Achieve

*You can always choose
to make it a good day*

I walked barefoot across my bedroom and peeked out the window searching for the morning sun. Not yet. Why should that not surprise me? George usually called before sunrise and he had just hung up. He was always spouting the importance of getting up with the roosters.

I must admit, the gift of intuition affirmations were empowering me and getting me fired up. My future was looking more rosy every day, so bye-bye sleeping in and hello new world. "Okay, Mr. Miracle Worker," I mumbled, "have it your way." I slipped into sweats and socks, stepped into my sneakers, and laced them up. Savoring the thought of another glorious autumn day in the mountains, I was ready to hike a favorite trail.

A few miles up the road and through an open gate leading into a lush forest, I parked my car on a dirt road beneath a giant cedar tree. I inhaled the dewy scent of the forest awakening to a new day. Walking toward a clearing flanked by a broken fence, crunching in the thick layer of needles beneath my feet, I wrapped my arms around my chest to create some warmth.

Performing my ritual deep breathing, stretches, and bends, an exasperated inner voice said, *C'mon, girl, get a move on.*

I sighed, inhaling the sweet scent of almond logs burning in a nearby house, and headed up the trail at an arm-swinging clip. The first part of the trail was a rigorous uphill climb, and I was wheezing when I got to the top ... so much for my fast pace. I kept telling myself that the best thing about going uphill was the return trip downhill. After twenty minutes I developed a groove, feeling jazzed about walking while enjoying the scenery. Dapples of sunlight dancing through fir branches illuminated the path, as gentle breezes whispered through the treetops. I paused to laugh at two squirrels chasing each other around the furrowed trunk of an old moss-covered cedar. Yes, this was my inspiration for the contents of the next envelope.

The house was quiet when I returned. Sheba was curled up asleep on the sofa and didn't even bother to get up and purr. Where was her usual "Hello, Mom, missed you. Glad you're back to feed me now"? She was probably so busy resenting me for waking her so early that she needed a nap. "Sheba, Mommy's home, and I'm the one who could use a nap about now." She wasn't impressed and didn't even open an eye. While I rubbed warmth back into my hands and watched her sleep, I decided I needed to get out more and talk with humans.

When I had last spoken with George, he hinted that A creates A. What did he mean—attitude, action, appreciation, abundance, what? Over the past few days, I had felt reassured that I was laying the groundwork to climb the mountain and swim upstream—ready to do whatever it would take to keep moving forward.

What I learned about myself surprised even me. I hadn't been that great of a student in high school or college, but I loved to learn now. When my grey matter was dormant, so was I. The gift of intuition was accelerating my momentum, and I was feeling more hopeful each day.

My first impulse was to bolt across the room and tear open the envelope, but since I was still shivering I decided to fix a cup of hot chocolate. I lit the fire under the kettle, opened the cupboard, and took out my favorite mug with cats on it. While impatiently waiting for the whistle to blow, I wandered around the kitchen and played back my messages. Had I heard that right? I ran back to the machine and hit the replay button. Yes, yes, yes, it was a meeting planner from Los Angeles requesting me to call her immediately about filling in for a speaker who had to cancel. Wonderful, a new client who wanted to book me for an audience of top corporate guns this weekend. Sure I could do that. My fingers dialed the number as fast as I could. It took less than a half hour to put all the details together. It was a done deal.

After I hung up I whooped so loud that Sheba had no choice but to wake up. She padded over, rubbed against my legs, and purred for a cat celebration treat. I smiled, knowing full well what a manipulator she was, and sprinkled some tuna tidbits into her dish. Watching her nibble I said, "Sheba, the gift of intuition must be working! Did you hear who that was? Thanks to a cancellation, I'm landing a speaking gig in L.A. Don't worry, your favorite sitter will take care of you." Shaking my head, I noticed that talking to my cat so much had me a bit concerned about my speaking skills with humans. The kettle whistled while I realized that cats were a tougher audience than humans any day of the week. I giggled as I leaned over to pick up the next envelope.

Day 15

Purpose

Purpose is the burning desire fueling the pursuit of a goal you wish to accomplish. It may be inspired by family, career, health, a sport, emotional or financial goals, and may change during different stages of your life.

An Olympic hopeful's purpose maybe to qualify for the team and earn one or more medals. Some parents aspire to pass certain qualities on to their children, such as self-reliance and love. Others find great reward in community service or building a church, and some see their purpose as creating financial abundance.

Enjoy today, but take time to revitalize your purpose; give thought as to why and where you want to be. Defining and then pursuing a worthy purpose will empower you to manifest greater rewards than you could ever imagine.

AFFIRMATION: I live with purpose.

Day 16
Work

Your work should create a sense of usefulness and accomplishment, along with financial reward. If you dislike your work, it becomes drudgery and steals your time and health. When work brings you enjoyment, you're creative and happy. Whatever work you do, embrace the experience and insights you gather along the way. Choose a career you like and go for it!

Remember, everything you learn has the potential to benefit you with your next endeavor. A waiter could run his own restaurant. A teacher may become a great motivator and change hundreds of lives. Be willing to take risks to discover the work you are destined to do.

AFFIRMATION: I enjoy my work.

Day 17

Knowledge

It's exciting to learn! Knowledge can enhance experience and build awareness. Seek out effective ways of expanding your knowledge through classes, CDs, books, the internet, or other people's expertise. Broaden your skill set by tackling a language, craft, volunteer activity, or computer class.

Informed citizens acquire knowledge that can empower them in protecting injustice, judgment, and discrimination. Seeking knowledge opens the mind to explore challenging new situations and possibilities. In difficult situations, knowledge gives you the leverage to make intelligent decisions.

Whether you're fifteen or seventy-five, knowledge empowers your choices. Make it a lifelong pursuit and a legacy to pass on to others.

AFFIRMATION: I expand my mind through knowledge.

Day 18

Communication

Communication covers how we express ourselves and receive information from others. There is no greater skill to build your confidence and move you up the career ladder than knowing what to say and how to say it.

Unfortunately, people spend less time developing their communication skills than they do watching their favorite television programs. When you communicate openly with family, friends, and co-workers, you encourage honest and fulfilling relationships. Be candid and positive, and speak and write with honesty and commitment.

Be a good listener by inviting people to express themselves and share information. Interactive communication encourages an exchange of thoughts and ideas that focus on solutions.

AFFIRMATION: I am an effective communicator.

Day 19

Consciousness

Consciousness is a state of awareness of one's thoughts and feelings. Higher levels of consciousness unite your soul with purpose, integrity, and virtue. Increasing your awareness helps you connect more effectively with other people. Consciousness promotes empathy, patience, tolerance, forgiveness, and understanding.

When searching for solutions, allow your consciousness to heighten your awareness and focus your attention on the highest good. Perception, alertness, kindness, sensitivity, emotional maturity, and thoughtfulness are all traits of a heightened spiritual consciousness.

AFFIRMATION: I trust my consciousness to enlighten me.

Day 20

Vision

To develop your vision, take a few moments each morning and evening to clearly visualize what you want and who you want to be. Through your daily meditations and affirmations, you can confirm what you ask for: health, abundance, adventure, and love. Feel, believe, and see your future. Ask if it is for your highest good. Live in the present with gratitude, and believe you are manifesting your vision. Through the power of visualization and dedication, you can become be an accomplished golfer, a great parent, or a business owner.

Envision your goals and impress them into your heart and mind. Then develop an action plan to make them real. Let your intuition guide you. Imagine what you want, be clear on why you want it, and then take action.

AFFIRMATION: I visualize the life I desire.

Day 21
Abundance

Abundance surrounds you and can be attracted to you in many different ways. Being thankful for all that you have rather than focusing on what you don't will help you keep a positive outlook. Your work and your expression of appreciation help manifest abundance.

You may believe the party is somewhere else when it's actually happening right now with you. People aren't born to live in poverty, but to love and live in joy, and to help one another do the same. Take a good look around and really see all that surrounds you. Do you have shelter, food, freedom of speech, libraries, and schools? Be thankful for your friends, family, pets, and all the blessings in your life. Be sure to thank the Universe for giving you the opportunity to work for what you want.

Abundance exists on all levels—financial, emotional, spiritual, and mental. Believe you are worthy of abundance and welcome it into your heart.

AFFIRMATION: I create abundance.

When the weekend arrived, I packed up my pages for the days I would be traveling and headed to the airport. My flight into Los Angeles had been delayed by mechanical problems. That was enough to unsettle my nerves. I had come to terms with being a plane crash survivor, and thereby a member of a very elite club that entitled me to be wary when I boarded an aircraft. Due to the delay, I arrived at the hotel around midnight. During the night I tossed and turned until the bed linens were in knots. I slept only three hours before the alarm sounded a wake-up signal. My nerves were jumping like grasshoppers because this was a crucial speech that could be a career maker or breaker.

The elegant entryway to the conference room was overflowing with flawlessly dressed executives clustered in groups, deep in conversation while sipping coffee from ceramic cups. As I looked at the latest Armani jackets and Chanel scarves, I straightened my dark, worn suit and felt for the small chain around my neck. Maybe I was out of touch with what was happening in the urban world. I had become a mountain gal. Hadn't George lectured me that you can't judge a book by the cover—*Everyone puts one pant leg on at a time.* He had emphasized that people the world over shared common hopes and dreams. I prayed he was right.

Scanning the room to verify the setup, I wondered if I was in the wrong conference hall, because it wasn't arranged the way I had requested. I stepped outside to check the sign on the door; sure enough, this was it. There was no raised platform, the podium had a fixed microphone instead of a handheld cordless one I had requested, and the narrow confines of the long room would make it difficult for people in the back to see me.

My watch indicated that only thirty minutes remained until the audience would take their seats. I felt a touch on my shoulder, and turned to encounter the meeting planner's smiling face.

"Hello, are you Donna?" she asked cheerfully. I nodded. "How are you?"

"I'm g ... great," I said with a stammer, "but I have a few quick questions. Is the room set up for my speech?"

"Well, yes. This is the best the hotel could come up with. I hope you can work with it."

The tightness in my chest heightened. "Do you think we can get a platform? Then the people in the back of the room can see me. Is there a handheld cordless microphone here so I can move around?"

She pursed her lips. "Hmm, let me call the hotel's technical department and see what they can do."

"Thank you so much; I'd really appreciate that."

By now, people were settling into their seats while I was anxiously counting the minutes left until my speech was scheduled to begin.

Ten minutes later she bustled in. "Sorry, Donna, no luck on the platform, but the hotel has a handheld microphone but it does have a cord. All their other microphones are in use."

I nodded, gritting my teeth. "Yes. Umm ... you made copies of my handouts? I don't see them on the chairs."

She lowered her brows and frowned over my question. "Handouts?"

The sinking feeling intensified. I knew I had overnight-mailed them to her, and she should have had them a few days ago. "Guess they got lost in the mail," I said, not wanting to further ignite the tension.

She gave me a put-on smile, prepared to walk away, and then turned. "Oh, I almost forgot, we're going to start you a little later because the president of the company requested a few minutes. Sorry, but I have to ask you to cut ten minutes from your speech."

My lungs suddenly seemed incapable of taking in air. We had agreed on a full hour for my presentation. Despair surged though me as my mind raced, rearranging my thoughts into some kind of order, trying to figure out what I could eliminate while still presenting an effective speech. Numb, I merely shook my head.

The meeting planner tilted her head to one side. "Just a quick point: you are presenting to directors, executives, and upper management."

My pulse jumped. What did she mean by emphasizing their importance? I wondered. Was I supposed to behave differently? "I understand," I said with a weak smile.

By now, panic was shredding my self-confidence to bits. What earthshaking message could I give to this cultivated audience? What I had to say was not budgetary or futuristic. My story was about a plane crash, and an Oklahoma man who mentors me in facing challenges head-on. Worse yet, I even talk about talking to my cat.

I poured a glass of water and sipped slowly. My panic escalated and my heart rhythm raced at a rapid thump-thump.

The company president stood at the podium and launched into his speech. I fidgeted through ten grueling minutes of cost-cutting rhetoric. He concluded his talk by announcing that year-end bonuses would be considerably less than previous years, and many departments would not issue bonuses at all. As the energy in the room bottomed out, the metallic taste of dread filled my mouth. How could I possibly captivate an audience that was obviously in shock? At least we had one thing in common: they were crashing and burning, and I planned to open my speech talking about a plane crashing and burning.

Rising slowly from my chair at the front of the room, I moved to the podium and unwound the microphone cord so I could be free to move around. From the time I began speaking, you could have heard a pin drop. I had the feeling that they weren't hearing me, but rather stewing over what the president had said. Even when I injected humor, there were only a few muffled chuckles from the crowd.

When I concluded my presentation, I was not expecting a standing ovation or massive applause, but I certainly didn't expect the uncomfortable silence that followed. Then, little by little, people began to applaud, but it never grew to more than a weak demonstration of courtesy. With barely enough time left to catch my flight home, I proceeded toward the exit, wishing that I could erase the event from my brain at once.

The meeting planner stopped me, shook my hand, and said, "I

believe you did a good job."

Believe. She believed I did a good job. Should I consider that a compliment? What did I believe? "Thanks," I said, thinking that one modest acknowledgment out of a hundred and fifty was better than none.

On the plane, I tried to delete the memory of how inadequate my speech had been. I became mesmerized by the shrinking landscape as I sat in a stupor, watching the buildings below vanish as rapidly as I felt my career would. My affirmations were ... well, let me say I didn't fulfill them this week: work, a flop; knowledge, a flop; communication, a big flop. All right, I created some abundance.

It was raining and windy when my flight landed in Reno, which suited my mood. The stormy weather would make the trip up through the mountains treacherous, so I waited inside the airport.

A gentleman smoking a pipe walked by and I felt that was a sign for me to call George. I thought about putting it off, but today was the day I was supposed to phone him. I dialed in his number and George picked up promptly.

In a chipper voice, he said, "Hi, Partner. How are you doing?"

A weak croak caught in my throat. "I landed in Reno. I'm calling from the airport."

"Sorry, didn't hear you. What was that again?"

Clearing my throat I repeated, "Landed in Reno. I'm at the airport. It's raining cats and dogs."

"You're not sounding too good, Partner. Are you sick?"

"Sick at heart. I've returned from what I hoped would be a career-making speech. These were bigwigs, George. The meeting was in Los Angeles. I flopped. They hated me."

He paused for a moment, then asked, "What makes you think those people didn't like what you had to say?"

"As you always say, you know when you know. They were upscale, prosperous executives, and everything went wrong." I continued. "The room setup was a nightmare. My handouts weren't copied so there was no material for my audience. My time slot was sliced by ten minutes only seconds before I went on. My ten minutes were then used by the company president to announce budgets were tightening and that bonuses would be cut. As far as applause, there wasn't any."

"Well, well, I would say you had some learning lessons today. All those curve balls must have rattled you. Sounds like your confidence took a beating."

I couldn't answer him. All I could think about was the humiliation I felt.

"Do you honestly think those executives already knew everything you said? Are you judging your success by how loud they applauded?"

"No. Well, maybe. I guess so. I don't know."

"Don't judge yourself," George insisted. "This was a test to see if you believe in yourself. Your purpose is to help people help themselves, and your message of hope applies to everyone from Fortune 500 executives to folks who work at the corner store."

"Yes, but why didn't they applaud? I think it's because what I said wasn't cutting edge information."

Silence came from the other end of the line. "You're running on negative energy, Partner. Remember the first affirmation you learned? Attitude!"

"Attitude," I mumbled.

"You need to change yours right now. I have some parting advice for you. Consider your last speech a lesson. Next time there may be some changes you want to make. Move on. Don't dwell on it. No one ever said being a speaker would be easy, or that every audience would be putty in your hands. I have a strong hunch that tomorrow will be a real eye-opener for you."

"I hope so," I said, still unsure of myself.

"Attitude. Attitude. Stop allowing other people's opinions to bring you down. You have to know who you are inside at all times. No one is perfect. Are you ready for your next hint about the gift of intuition?"

"George, I never even figured out the last hint, A and A."

"You lived it today: Act and Achieve. Now here's your new hint. It's about excitement, spirit, and gusto. It's getting late. Time for me to go."

"Wait, I don't understand ... it." I stopped talking when I heard the dial tone.

Journal
Act and Achieve

What did my mother always say? "Don't count your chickens before they are hatched." Did I go into that speech cocky and thinking I would WOW them? Or was I set up by circumstances that caused me to fail? Hmm ... this will take some time to fully comprehend.

I was paid great money for the speech, yet I feel awful. What I need to do is manifest balance—giving a good speech and having the audience understand my presentation has value. Also, getting paid for a good job. A standing ovation ... no, don't go there Donna, stay with an outstanding speech that helps people. No ego!

There I was, moving along at a nice pace and POW! I feel like the rug was pulled out from under me. My spiritual awareness is imperative if I am going to deal with these challenges. If I had a real grip on my intuition and trusted it, I would have known what to do. Give me a sign, please, give me a sign. Okay ... even a signal would be great. How about a hint? Is anyone listening up there? Last request: give me anything. WAIT. That's all I'm feeling, WAIT.

I sat with the journal in my hands for a long time and all I could feel was "wait"—nothing else. Finally I made a decision to review the affirmations starting with Day 1: attitude, all the way to abundance, and see if that helped. I glanced up at the ceiling. I could use some help! Any time now.

Purpose
Work
Knowledge
Communication
Consciousness
Vision
Abundance

Chapter Eleven
Live Your Passion

It's your passion that ignites the energy
to move you from thought to action

The morning after my ill-fated speech, I trudged up the steps to my office with a lethargic feeling plaguing my legs that weighed them down like lead. Collapsing into my chair, I was about to check my e-mail when the phone startled me.

Forcing a smile, I summoned up a cheerful greeting. "Hartley International, this is Donna. How may I help you?"

A familiar-sounding voice at the other end responded, "Donna, good morning, this is Ted Johnson."

"Ted Johnson?" I squeaked as I bolted upright. My head started to pound. I was afraid he was going to ask for a refund for my speech. He was the company president who spoke yesterday. I swallowed hard, searching for something to say, when he continued, "First of all, I want to apologize. By taking your time away to give my people the bad news about their bonuses right before your presentation, I put you in a tough position."

The palpitations in my chest eased up a bit as I blurted out, "Uh ... huh."

"Second, I want to say that you did an outstanding job. It took courage to admit you are a work in progress. Your Miss Hawaii story was incredible. The plane crash ordeal was an eye-opener. While you were speaking, I know now that most of the audience was thinking about their shrinking bonuses. You pointed out that the most productive way to overcome challenges is to learn and grow. You made me realize it's time our company makes some changes, too."

Was I hearing him right? "I'm delighted you felt my speech had significance. Thank you so much for your call."

After I'd hung up I sat staring into space, replaying in my mind everything he had said. Slowly, I swiveled my chair around toward the computer with fingers flying over the keyboard. Scanning over my inbox, I noticed two unfamiliar names. Curious, I opened the first message and read:

I was in your audience yesterday. What you said had a powerful effect on me. I drove home at night thinking I wasn't living the life I wanted. I was neglecting my marriage. I shared your story with my wife. We both have been taking each other for granted. After talking things through for a long time, we agreed to work on our relationship. Every day, like you said.

Thank you,

Ben

I read Ben's e-mail again. I had assumed the audience wasn't listening to me. I opened the next message:

I don't know if you remember seeing me, but I sat in the front row wearing a navy blue suit, and have shoulder-length brown hair. I know plenty about the technical aspects of my job, but my people skills and attitude could use some improvements. I've been passed over for promotion and wasted time blaming other people. I wanted to let you know I'm thinking seriously about what it would take for my advancement and how I can work to improve my interpersonal skills to become more personable.

Thank you and God bless.
Susan B.

I jumped up out of my chair and danced around the center table in my office. I stretched my arms toward the ceiling, laughing and whooping for joy. After a few minutes of shameless abandon, I came to a dead stop, remembering my last conversation with George. He insisted it's not up to other people to make me feel good, but I needed to know I was doing the best job I could. Confidence ... not there yet. Had to work on that. When George spent the day with me at Lake Tahoe and we were in the coffee shop, he explained how I had to **feel it.** If I wasn't on target with my emotions, I would have no energy. WOW, so true! He also mentioned that this day would be insightful. He was right on all accounts.

Making a mad dash down the stairs, taking two at a time, I burst into the kitchen and grabbed the next envelope. When I read the title, "Live Your Passion," I chortled. "Mr. Miracle Worker, you have so much wisdom." Opening the envelope and removing the enclosed pages, I laid them out on the table and began to read.

Day 22

Passion

Do what you love and believe in who you are. It's your passion that ignites the energy to move from thought to action. Martin Luther King, Jr., Louis Pasteur, and Mother Teresa were passionate people who believed in their work, and their dedication altered history. Let them serve as role models; live and love with boundless enthusiasm.

Are you committed to your relationships, work, and a healthy lifestyle? If not, take a long hard look at what is holding you back from realizing your desires. Is fear from your past preventing you from kindling the fires of passion? If so, let go of the past and live in the present. What do you want in your life? Go for it now. Every day is a new adventure. Live each one with gusto.

AFFIRMATION: I live with passion.

Day 23
Family

When you interact with your family, treat them with gentleness, kindness, respect, and love. A loving family environment provides a safe haven where you can belong. It's a place of refuge where hugs are plentiful, common interests are shared, and feelings are talked through.

When the outside world becomes lonely and fragmented, we turn to our family for comfort, safety, and understanding. We benefit from shared wisdom, resources, and support. If you make a mistake or are harsh, apologize. Keep the lines of communication open. No one is perfect. Sometimes it is difficult but be forgiving and accepting. Unconditional love and deep bonding are the rare gifts a family can give.

AFFIRMATION: I love my family.

Family ... I read the title to the affirmation again. *Family. It's a place of refuge where hugs are plentiful, common interests are shared and feelings are talked through.* Oh brother, that was a list of things I was not living. *Will I ever heal with my family? Will I? I really would like to heal.*

I knew my family loved me in their own way, but maybe because they couldn't be there for me, I was sent George. Interesting. I put the piece of paper down and went on to the next self-talk.

Day 24

Compassion

Compassion is a pure form of emotion. It heals relationships, raises self-esteem, and is a caring legacy to pass on from generation to generation. When you are compassionate, you identify with others from deep within yourself.

Being compassionate means listening when a friend is going through a tough time and being patient when someone has difficulty making a decision. Looking beyond your own needs and being of service to others is one of the greatest comforts you can give to another living being.

Practicing empathy awakens your heart and soul to the boundless joy of spiritual awareness. Although extremely challenging at times, it is well worth the effort to practice acts of kindness and compassion.

AFFIRMATION: I am compassionate.

Day 25

Persistence

Persistence is having the tenacity to move forward through obstacles and disappointments. It is often the difference between failure and success. Many people fall short in their lives because they do not open their hearts and minds to the gifts of inner strength and perseverance.

Sales studies indicate it takes five or more interactions to make a sale, yet many people give up after the first rejection. Persistence makes the difference between drafting an outline of a book and publishing it, or taking a few classes and earning a degree. You could hit a few tennis balls or you could become an excellent tennis player. It takes practice and persistence.

When you believe in yourself, abundance and fulfillment follow. Being *persistent expands your confidence and helps you achieve your dreams.*

AFFIRMATION: I am persistent.

Day 26

Change

Confronting change means overcoming your fears and taking action. Change is an opportunity to stretch yourself and grow beyond your comfort zone. Change does not guarantee you will be successful in all your endeavors, but is an ever-present dynamic you must learn to accept.

Choosing to live a life of quiet desperation filled with fear of change keeps you forever wondering what life would be like if only you had tried something different. Four of the saddest words are, "I should have tried."

The challenge to change and grow as an individual can lead to very rewarding experiences. Although sometimes scary and seemingly insurmountable, change is often forced upon you, but the benefit of taking on transformation is spiritual growth.

Look forward with self-respect and confidence toward what you will accomplish.

AFFIRMATION: I embrace change as an opportunity.

Day 27

Creativity

Your creativity is an expression of your originality. It is your unique imagination that makes your dreams and desires come alive. Have the courage to explore your creative potential and expand its boundaries through training, coaching, and education. Who knows, you might possess the qualities to become a master painter or perfect a family recipe and turn it into a successful business. The sky is the limit.

How do you discover your creativity? Relax in a quiet place, close your eyes, unwind, and allow your stream of consciousness to go to work. Think about what you like to do, what inspires you and brings you joy. Jot your ideas down and open up your imagination to all the possibilities life offers.

Focus on one or two talents you enjoy. Visualize yourself following through by purchasing the supplies, signing up for a class, or designing a space where you can bring your world of ideas to life. Then, commit energy and time to express your talents. Creativity enriches your life.

AFFIRMATION: I am creative.

Day 28
Manifestation

Manifestation is the ability to attract what you desire in life. By determining what you want to manifest and clarifying if it is for your highest good, you can outline your goals. The ideal way to begin the process is through meditation. Calm yourself in a quiet place, light a candle, play soft music or listen to a guided CD, and ask to connect to a higher source.

In your quiet state of mind, explore what it is that brings you joy and best serves your highest purpose. Take note of the answer that comes to you. Once you know what you want, focus on it and visualize your life as though you already have it. You may manifest a home, fulfillment in a career, or a loving relationship with your child. Then, work for it. Most importantly, be grateful for what you have and what is yet to come to you.

Using the skills of visualization and self-talk, remember that saying or *thinking positive thoughts will draw to you what you desire. God didn't put you on the earth to suffer. Live with purpose and attract what you want through manifestation.*

AFFIRMATION: I manifest my highest good.

Showered, dressed, but shoeless, I pulled up the window shade to reveal a glorious sight: a sunrise rosy as a ripe apple and brilliant as spun gold. More and more I understood why my mentor always said to rise and shine early in the morning.

In the kitchen, I assembled all the ingredients for my third energy protein shake of the week. While sipping it, I sat down and dialed George's number. When he answered, I said with an accent, "Ay, it's gonna to be a great day, mate, wouldn't ya say so?"

"That's new." He laughed. "You sound unusually perky for this hour of the morning."

"I guess the gift of intuition is sinking in, unless I've transformed into a rooster."

"No guessing about it," he declared. I heard a match being struck, followed by the familiar sound of George drawing on his pipe. "That's why we're here, to comprehend our life lessons. Tell me, what have you learned in the last few weeks?"

"Ask me an easy question." I groaned. Where should I begin? Thoughts swirled around in my head while I attempted to put them in some order.

"For starters, this week was powerful. You won't believe it, but the president of the company I spoke for called and apologized for the difficult position he'd put me in. He even said that my presentation was outstanding and had inspired him to make some needed changes."

"Uh-huh. Patience is pretty powerful stuff," declared the Duke of Georgeism.

"I thought he was calling for his money back but ..."

"Donna, you've got to believe in yourself. What else have you learned?"

"Those little affirmations got me thinking—passion, family, persistence, change, and to top it off, manifestation. What I thought was love was my neediness manifesting itself. I was so afraid of not having a man, and of being alone, that I sacrificed my own happiness." Pausing to collect my thoughts I continued, "I want a daughter more than anything else in this world, and I thought it was necessary to be in a traditional marriage."

"Your presumption that only a conventional lifestyle would be acceptable was blocking you. Trust your intuition. So what are you visualizing now?"

"I'm seeing my daughter coming to me. I'm not sitting around waiting for a bundle to be left on my doorstep, or planning a walk down the aisle in white. I've made three phone calls regarding adoption and I'm going to make more inquiries this week. First on my agenda is figuring out the costs involved and filling out reams of paperwork. George, when you were in Tahoe you told me that part of the process was to **visualize it.**"

Laughing heartily he said, "God bless us all when you're a mom because your daughter is going to be just like you, a pistol! Keep up the good work, meditate, and visualize your daughter with you."

George continued, "When I was a young boy, my father would get me up before the rooster crowed. I gotta tell you, I couldn't think of anything worse, especially as a teenager. He'd make me meditate every morning. Sometimes I'd sit there pouting, not thinking about anything but sleeping. After awhile though, I started to clear my mind, allowing my creativity to surface and seeing new possibilities. The answers became more apparent to me. Don't let a day go by without creating some quiet time. Meditation clears the way for intuition, and trusting your intuition brings the knowing. Got it?"

"Yes, George, I've got it. You have told me this story before."

"I guess you are going to hear it until you get it."

"Honest, I got it."

It makes my day to hear that. Well, Partner, I need to be heading out soon. What do you have planned for today?"

"I'm driving to Mill Valley," I said. "That's right outside San Francisco near the Golden Gate Bridge."

"Oh, I like that city, but I haven't been there in quite some time. Are you working?"

"No, I wish I was. I'm going to a nursing home to visit my good friend Brad. He has multiple sclerosis and is not doing well. His wife, Isa, called, and I could tell from her voice that it was time for me to visit."

"Well, that's mighty fine," George said. He became quiet and I heard him inhale, then exhale. I envisioned him at the other end, cherry tobacco smoke circling his head like a halo, eyes squinting. After what seemed to be five minutes, he cleared his throat.

"So are you ready to see what's in the last envelope? I'd normally play a little guessing game with you, but since you've worked so hard I'm going to flat out tell you what's in the envelope. I saved the best two for last: Love and Life."

How ironic, I thought, and snickered. "For me, this should be interesting. I flunked love more times than I can count."

"True enough, but things are going to change."

I sat straight up. "What do you mean, change? How? When?"

"I'm not letting you bait me, Partner. Have a great visit with your friends. I'd surely like to come along and meet them. Maybe I will. I like the feeling I get when you talk about them. Yep, maybe I will. Gotta go. Start working on the last two affirmations and I'll talk to you next week."

"George, what do you mean you will come along and visit? George? George ...?"

Journal
Live Your Passion

*S*omebody famous must have come up with this quote, "Life is a roller coaster ride." My life certainly is. One day I'm up, the next I'm crashing, and the following day I'm loving life again. Listen, God, sorry—please listen, God, this is the deal: my goal is to be BALANCED. Day 10 was all about balance, and I'm learning to comprehend the importance of that little affirmation.

Passion is another story; I want it, I yearn for it, I love it. I choose to live a life that is passionate. Let me count my blessings that I'm passionate about: living in the mountains near a beautiful lake, my career, my friends, snow skiing, my home, travel, George, and of course, my bloomin'cat. Almost forgot, thank you, God, from my heart for being there for me.

I am very passionate about the daughter who will come to me. I wonder how I'll know if she is the right child for me. More importantly, I wonder how Sheba the queen will adjust to another high-maintenance female in the house. I'll review the affirmations of the week, and concentrate on each word.

Passion
Family
Compassion
Persistence
Change
Creativity
Manifestation

Chapter Twelve
Love Your Life

Life is an exciting adventure
filled with opportunities

Dressed in jeans and a warm sweater, I felt the chill in the air as sparkling frost coated the landscape. It was a four-hour drive to Mill Valley, and I basked in the quiet with only the steady hum of the engine to keep me company. My friend Isa had phoned me the day before and though she made every effort to sound cheerful, I could hear the fatigue and despair in her voice.

It was about her husband Brad. She was afraid he wasn't going to live much longer. After years of tireless support, Isa was exhausted and on the verge of a breakdown. I sensed her gratitude when I told her I'd come down for a visit.

While driving, I reminisced about Brad when he was healthy and full of spunk. Then I tried to brace myself to be ready to see him as he was today: confined to a hospital bed, frail and helpless. Why was he stricken in his thirties with multiple sclerosis? What was he supposed to learn from all this? My mind drifted back to when I had known

Brad in Tahoe and he was an avid tennis player, snow skier, and couldn't live without his Harley. His dream was to own a motorcycle shop; all he needed was the money. He gambled on a shortcut, a quick score. A friend tempted him with a one-time windfall for smuggling drugs into the country. His dream of owning a motorcycle shop vanished when he was caught at the border. He spent years in prison and it took a toll on his body. Was it a karmic lesson?

After he served his time, Brad told me that he had met the most wonderful woman in the world, Isa, and that they were going to be married. It had been a long time since I had heard Brad so full of life. A few days before their wedding, he'd been diagnosed with MS. They wouldn't let this disease stand in the way of their love. An aura of love radiated around them at their wedding.

Bordering Mill Valley on Highway 101, I put my thoughts aside and focused on the picturesque surroundings. The trees were vibrant with the orange, red, and gold colors of fall. Although there was a cold breeze, the lush green grass had been spared from frostbite. Far in the distance, like an icon peeking through the mist, I could see the Golden Gate Bridge gracefully spanning the bay. The beauty of the day played a stark contrast to the drab institution of the nursing home where Isa's and Brad's love had been tested in every imaginable way. Yet they were more devoted to each other now than when they first fell in love. The sheer irony of it struck me. Here I was pondering love and life, the last two affirmations, and about to visit two people who taught me so much about both.

Sadly, battling Brad's illness over the years had depleted all their money. So when his condition deteriorated beyond home care, it became necessary for him to enter a state-run nursing home. The lobby inside the dreary institution featured bare walls and brown industrial-grade carpet. The air was stale and the distinct, acrid scent of urine permeated the building. Eight sets of vacant-eyed patients in wheelchairs were assembled in the lobby, with one slack-mouthed man leaning so far over the side of his chair that his hand dragged on the floor. Definitely a health care system in trouble, I thought. My heart ached.

As I turned down the hall toward Brad's room I spotted Isa's curly blond hair and slender body bent over the water fountain, filling a plastic pitcher. Her shoulders seemed even more stooped than I remembered. The complications of Brad's illness were taking a toll on her.

"Hey, good lookin'," I piped up.

Isa turned, her face brightening as she threw her arm over my shoulders. "Donna! I'm happy you made it. I've been counting the minutes. You don't know how much I appreciate you coming," she said, stepping back, tears welling in her eyes.

Isa had never been one to keep her emotions politely concealed. She wore her heart on her well-worn sleeve. Grabbing my hand she murmured, "I'm glad we have a few minutes alone to talk. I want you to read this note Brad gave me."

She removed a folded paper from her pocket and handed it to me. I took the note, unfolded it, and read:

I love you more than I ever thought I could. I know the feeling is genuine because I've never felt anything like this before. You have always been my inspiration.

Our anniversary is coming soon, my darling, and I am praying for something special to give you.

Love, Brad

I refolded the note, tracing the well-worn creases, and returned it to Isa. "It's beautiful. He loves you so much."

"He asked one of the nurses to write it. These few words mean so much to me. I've read it many times. You've been such a dear friend over the years I wanted to share it with you." Isa said softly, "Did you know the flowers you sent arrived on our anniversary? The day he gave me the note, the flowers arrived."

I fumbled for words. I mumbled, "I had no idea it was your anniversary. I sent them because you were both in my thoughts." Then I smiled to myself because I thought, *You know when you know.* I had been developing my intuition and it was working. I was thinking about Brad and Isa but the most important thing, George would say, is acting upon the thought, and I did.

"Let's go see Brad. He's so excited about you visiting," Isa said, hooking her arm in mine.

We walked down the corridor and paused before an open door. I steeled myself and stepped into Brad's room. The once vibrant man with the intense blue gaze, blond hair, and a killer smile had been replaced by a sunken face and frail body. My emotions sank like dead weight in my stomach as I pulled myself together and walked over to the side of his bed. His blue eyes twinkled.

"You know, I could spot those blue eyes of yours in a room full of Scandinavians."

Brad feebly motioned. "Come closer, Donna, and let me get a good look at you." Sitting on the bed I took his hand in mine. "It's great to see you." He glanced up at Isa and in that instant I witnessed the unconditional love between them.

"Tell me about your life and what's happening in Tahoe," he insisted.

Very ironic that I came here to visit Brad and he was concerned about me. I quickly caught him up on what was going on in my world. "Enough about me now, how goes it with you?"

Forming his words slowly he said, "If I could wish for anything, I'd climb out of this bed, stand on my own two feet, and wrap my legs around my old Harley. I'd tear up the highway full throttle." He caught his breath. "I'd feel the wind blowing in my face, smell the air, and have the ride of my life." He sighed. "Oh, how I miss that." He turned with a loving glance toward Isa. "Then I'd walk barefoot on the beach with my wife." He paused to catch his breath. "The tide would be in, washing between our toes." He gasped for air.

He beckoned Isa to move in closer. Slowly and with difficulty he continued, "The sun." Brad stared at his wife. "It turned the sky that silky orange when we were on the beach?"

Isa nodded, tearing up.

He rested a few moments before continuing, "I'd hug, kiss and tell you I love you until you were sick of hearing it."

Isa held his hand. "Never. I'd never get tired of hearing it."

"See why I have the best wife in the world?" He had trouble forming his words as he continued. Slowing, he said, "Isa keeps telling me how handsome I am. There was a time in my life when I worried about how I looked, but today, it's not important." Again he rested before he spoke. "Now all I care about is what happens to my wife," Brad said as he struggled to breathe.

"Honey, if I had wings, I would carry you to God and ask him to keep you safe in the light," Isa said.

Overcome with emotion, I blinked back the tears. Did I even need to read my new affirmations? I was living them. Love ... this was its truest form, not what I had experienced with men. Life ... Brad was fighting for his with every breath. I felt overwhelming compassion as I watched Isa lie down on the hospital bed beside Brad to calm him. He had expended so much energy on the conversation that he was tiring.

Isa ran her fingers through his hair. "Brad, you can close your eyes if you're tired. I'm right here. I love you."

I was privileged to witness what George had taught me: **think it, feel it, visualize it, say it, do it**, and you'll own it. Love.

How beautiful life is
when you live in the moment

A stern-faced nurse marched into the room. With her faded

uniform, sensible shoes, and tightly wrapped hair she sent a clear message, "Don't mess with me."

"Medication, Brad," she growled, tossing me an impatient look.

His eyes lit up with a mischievous twinkle as he said, "Have I told you how good you look today?"

A smile actually parted her thin lips and she softened before my eyes. There was a special gentleness in her touch as she fluffed Brad's pillow, and a gentle manner as she helped him swallow several pills.

"Oh Brad, you say that every day, and to all the nurses."

"That's right, because I can't help it. Everyone looks good to me."

I glanced at Brad's pallid face and understood how difficult it was for him to form a smile. He wasn't the great tennis player, or the daredevil skier, or the foolhardy motorcyclist any longer. Brad was a compassionate, loving, and accepting human being.

I glimpsed the powerful spirit within that kept Brad from caving in. Although the outside had deteriorated, the inside had blossomed into a wonderful soul. Kissing him goodbye, I accepted Isa's offer to walk with me back to the lobby.

"Donna," she said sadly as we walked arm in arm, "I love him so much."

"I know."

Sitting in my car, I couldn't move, couldn't put the key in the ignition, couldn't muster up the strength to drive. The onslaught of San Francisco traffic was too much for me to face. There was only silence as tears rolled down my cheeks.

I inhaled, then sniffed, and sniffed again. What was that familiar smell? I looked left, then to my right, then turned around and glanced at the back seat of my car, then up at the roof. Firmly holding the steering wheel, I sniffed again and smelled George's cherry pipe tobacco. Is this what he meant when he said he'd come along to meet my friends?

"George ... George ... is that you? George, are you here? Am I imagining this ... or are you really here?" The cherry pipe tobacco and George was what I thought about on my drive back to Tahoe.

I finally arrived home and opened the last envelope. There were only two affirmations, but I had the feeling it would take me awhile to get a handle on them.

Day 29

Love

Love is a deep, tender feeling of affection that allows you to express compassion and tenderness. You first must love yourself to be able to love others. Always know that God loves you as you are. Be more patient and tolerant of yourself.

True love demonstrates emotional and mature growth. When you genuinely love someone, you encourage them to be all they can be. We gain insight from different kinds of love: romantic love, love for parents, siblings, children, friends, and love of oneself.

When you have love, it adds value to your life; you're healthier, less stressed, more confident, and you open your life to kindness, friendship, and laughter. Love without judgment. Love is the greatest commitment we can make to the Universe, ourselves, and others.

AFFIRMATION: I love unconditionally.

Day 30

Life

Life encompasses the spiritual, mental, and physical experiences of your existence. Every day brings newness. The quality of your life is determined by the choices you make, the people you associate with, and the knowledge you gain from your experiences. Circumstances and situations in life are not always fair, but you are in control of how you allow these things to affect your attitude and values. By focusing on your appreciation of family and friends and consistently expressing gratitude, you will create a meaningful life.

We all face obstacles and challenges from time to time. It's how you react that determines the outcome. You are an individual like no other. You maintain your own set of fingerprints and no one else has your biography. You have been gifted with special talents to benefit yourself and others. Life is an opportunity for you to contribute to the world—become a teacher, volunteer, mentor, nurse, an inventor, or whatever your calling may be. The important thing is to explore your potential and grow your talents. The reward for your efforts will be an abundant life. Live in the moment. Love, laugh, and live your destiny.

AFFIRMATION: I live each day to the fullest.

I finished Day 30 and needed some air, so I decided to go outside and deal with my firewood. Nothing like hard labor to burn off the stress. I tossed the last two logs onto the impressive stack of firewood in my side yard, tugged off my gloves, and stepped back to assess my handiwork. It was very comforting to know I would have more than enough wood for the cold winter ahead. Extending my arms over my head to stretch my aching back, I realized it was quitting time. An autumn chill lingered in the air, prodding me to bring a load of logs into the house.

With Sheba curled up beside me and a warm, crackling fire to ward off the cold, I settled in for a peaceful evening. On my lap sat all the envelopes enclosing the gift of intuition. Thirty little bits and pieces of wisdom written down to kick start my body, mind, and spirit and get me fired up. The last two affirmations played havoc with my thought process. Here I was in my forties, and I was pondering the true meaning of the words love and life. This was a difficult concept for me to grasp because I had mistaken love for affection, sex, or an activity calendar. Was I capable of being loved and giving love?

"Maybe I'm not!" My words were so loud I startled Sheba. Feeling my distress, she climbed onto my lap, purring loudly, insisting I calm down. My chest was rising and falling as whimpering sounds came out of my mouth. "If I'm not able to love ... no one will want me. I won't be capable of loving my daughter."

Sheba placed her paws squarely on my chest as she gently licked my face, willing me to focus on her. With every lick she seemed to calm me down. Her blue eyes reassured me, *I love you.* Holding her tightly and rocking her from side to side I whispered, "What is this life about? Why am I here? What am I supposed to do?"

 ## Journal
Love and Life

Journal, journal, journal. Do you do any good? I write in you night after night, and I'm still waiting for some enlightened moments of WISDOM. Excuse me, where are they? Let me just tell you how things are. I'm supposed to be raising my cat, but why do I have the feeling she's raising me?

So many questions. Because of the knowledge George has given me, I now know I am responsible for everything I create. WOW, that is a full-time job. There are parts of my life I do not like. So God, are you listening? Thank you for everything but I've got some changes in mind. Can I alter what I don't like about my life? I guess the real question is: I know I can change some things, but will I fall back into my old patterns again? Can I turn my weaknesses into my strengths?

Will I be able to develop my intuition and trust it all the time? And, as Mr. Wise Man insists, someday will my intuition guide me to the knowing? You know when you know. What does he really mean by that little phrase?

Before I go, I have one more question. Will I have enough money to pay all my bills on time? Just asking. So keep me working.

Love
Life

Part III

A Wish Fulfilled

Chapter Thirteen
The Truth Beyond

Meditation is the stuff of miracles

The first snowstorm of the season had carpeted my yard in fleecy white and in its wake emerged a day of dazzling winter splendor. I straightened up from shoveling, massaged my back, and willed away the pain. It was one of the many times my back seemed determined to remind me that I had survived a major plane accident.

When I heard the phone ringing, I gratefully dropped the shovel and dashed into the house, stomping snow from my boots and tugging off my heavy gloves. "Hello," I said breathlessly into the phone.

"Hello yourself, Partner," replied a familiar voice.

It was George. *How odd that he's calling in the afternoon*, I thought. He always rang first thing in the morning. My second thought was undeniable guilt for waiting so long to call him. "Hi, George! It's great to hear from you."

"I was getting worried, haven't heard from you in a while. I thought you were going to let me know how you were progressing with the gift of intuition."

"I know. Sorry," I apologized, "but I haven't been avoiding you on purpose. These last two affirmations, the love stuff and the life stuff, threw me for a loop. I'm afraid I screwed up my life more than I want to admit. Bouncing like a pinball with no focus and still expecting results."

"Well then, I think it's time we talk through those feelings," he said. "I do want to see you in person. The good news is I have business in San Francisco. Let me check my schedule; I've got it right here."

I heard papers shuffling, and then George announced, "I'm going to be in San Francisco in three weeks, December 17 to be exact. I'm staying near Fisherman's Wharf and I happen to have that entire afternoon off. How about driving down to meet me? You name the place for lunch."

"Oh, I'd love it. Let's meet at Pier 39—it's really close by. It's Christmas time and at the entrance they'll have a gigantic Christmas tree with gorgeous decorations and presents with designer bows beneath. There are benches nearby, so we can meet at the tree."

"That'll be a first, but it sounds promising," George quipped. "How about noon for lunch?"

"Perfect. I have a great restaurant in mind." I was also delighted that I would have some time before we met—enough time to delve deeper, nail down the more challenging affirmations and embed them in my mind.

"Okay, Partner. I'll see you December 17 at twelve o'clock, right by the glorious tree."

Hanging up the phone, I donned my gloves and returned to shoveling. Half an hour later, back inside and warming myself by the fireplace, I kept eyeing the envelopes stacked on the coffee table. Time to read them again. My new convictions catapulted to the forefront of my mind: *Manage your attitude and you manifest the outcome.*

* * * *

San Francisco's Golden Gate Bridge is a magnificent structure embedded in the rocky shoreline abutted against a city of well-kept Victorians and skyscrapers. As I turned onto the street parallel to the marina, I opened the window to inhale the refreshing ocean air.

The Marina Green was alive with exercise enthusiasts lifting weights and joggers performing warm-up stretches. Cool sea breezes swept a colorful cluster of Chinese box, dragon, and other animal-shaped kites across the sky.

Enchanted by the animated sight, I steered my car down the street leading to Ghirardelli Square, maneuvered it closer to the water, and caught the pervasive odor of fish. After circling around half a dozen times, it must have been my day because I found parking and it was free. I checked my watch. Right on time.

It was easy to spot George leaning back on a bench, looking relaxed, with the familiar wisps of smoke rising from his beloved pipe. He was enjoying his favorite pastime: observing people. I slid in next to him. "Sir, is this seat taken?"

Glancing at me, he removed his pipe and smiled warmly. "Well, Partner, it's good to see you."

"You too." Wrapping my arms around him, I held him tight. Then we gazed for a while at the parade of people walking by, some dressed in black leather and sporting multicolored spiked hair, and others looking like typical Christmas shoppers.

"Well, Partner," he said, rising from the bench, "my tummy is growling for some good, hearty food. What do you say we go find some?"

Grinning, I jumped to my feet. "I know, feed you first. As a matter of fact, I'm taking you to a quaint place with a million-dollar view: the Swiss House." I glanced in the direction of the restaurant. "We'd better get moving. It's a bit of a walk."

As we strolled along the pier, George sized up a rambunctious teenager sporting a hat with a Hells Angels insignia. Then he turned his twinkling eyes on me. "So, did you finish the gift of intuition?"

I wasn't ready to discuss this yet, and opted for distraction instead. Pausing at a vendor's stand, I tugged on George's sleeve and waved some herbal bath salts under his nose. "They're to die for, aren't they?"

He took a big whiff and made a face. "You actually bathe in this stuff? Smells like salad dressing to me," he grumbled.

I giggled. When we came to the entertainment stage, we paused to watch street performers putting on a show. A sword-swallower left me covering my eyes. "Yuck!"

The next act was a young mime who captured my attention with his exaggerated gestures and farcical facial expressions.

George gestured. "It's a talent to be able to get your point across without saying a word. In fact, that's what I'd like to talk about today—ways to communicate without speaking."

"Me, not talk?"

"That's right; you don't need to talk to have people understand you."

"Interesting, Mr. Miracle Worker."

"Yes, you not talk." He gave me a look that indicated he was thinking why had *he* been assigned to look after me. I was always a work in progress.

When we stepped inside the restaurant, George glanced around. "Oh yes. This is my kind of place. If the food is half as good as the view, you'll have made me a happy man."

Our window table overlooked a herd of playful sea lions. Farther out, on an isolated island sat the grim bastion of Alcatraz prison. It was an ominous sight to behold through the mist wafting up from the water. Inside, fire blazed in an open pit, and I gauged by George's satisfied smile that he was pleased with his surroundings.

I watched his eyes skim the surface of the sea and rest on the island. "So that's the notorious Alcatraz. If only those walls could talk. Some hard lessons were learned there."

"Speaking of lessons George, it's time to celebrate! I'm still alive. I finished the intuitive program, all thirty days. In fact, I read them over and over again. Granted, I'm not exactly rolling in dough yet, nor do I have a daughter, and there's the man thing: void."

George shook his head. "That's enough on that topic."

He signaled for the waiter. "Two steaming hot Irish coffees with real whipped cream on top."

Picking up a piece of warm sourdough bread I said, "Better get this in my stomach before the drinks arrive." George chuckled.

When the waiter brought our food, George eyed my crab salad, then glanced down at his plate heaped with broiled halibut, creamed potatoes, and a vegetable mix drenched in butter.

"You should have ordered my lunch," he chided. "That plateful of leaves you're eating wouldn't keep a rabbit alive. You'll need strength to work through your lessons."

I rolled my eyes and blurted out, "George, fat is not strength."

"You've got that one right," he said after swallowing a forkful of creamed potatoes. "Genuine strength comes from the inside, not the outside."

He considered me from across the table. "I'm glad you decided to meet me today. I've wanted to talk to you about your intuition. You must comprehend the importance of intuition and your ability to act on it. This is a life skill. Your assignment is to live it every day. It will save your life."

George paused and stared at me. I wanted to comment on what he had said but nothing would come out of my mouth. He continued, "The affirmations keep you focused on the present. Why, I've heard you laugh more today than you have in months. That's a good sign if ever I've heard one. Now, let's take some time to rehash my visit to

Tahoe. Okay, **think it**; remember the crawdad lesson?"

I chuckled. "Of course I do. I believed the bait and where I was sitting were the reasons I didn't catch many crawdads. Negative thoughts were my problem."

George smiled. "Well stated. Do you remember the next level and the lesson behind it?"

"**Feel it**," I said gingerly. "That warm, cozy coffee shop with the delicious pastries, mmmm ... I can taste it now."

He cleared his throat. "Let's get back to reality."

"The couple next to us was arguing instead of understanding each other. It's all about love, isn't it?" I asked as I looked at George.

He wiped his plate clean with a crust of bread and sat back with a contented sigh. "It's like stirring up an Irish stew with love and light as the meat and potatoes. Then you sprinkle in kindness and patience, then add a dash of appreciation and joy. Whip all that up together and you have a pot full of life that's perfect in every way."

"You have lived on the farm too long," I kidded.

I fell silent for a moment, thinking back to our discussion at Fanny Bridge in Tahoe City. "**Visualize it**, that was a tough one for me. I couldn't turn off the outside world long enough to focus. Do you have any secrets you can share with me to help overcome my resistance?"

He thought for a moment. Then his eyes lit up. "Matter of fact, I do. I'm going to give you the four A's to help you visualize what you want.

- One is *Assessment*—discovering what it is you really need.

- Two is *Alignment*—focusing your energy through meditation.

- Three is *Action*—taking positive steps.

- Four is *Accountability*—being responsible for your actions.

The clearer your vision, the quicker you'll manifest it and draw it to you."

George paused. "Let's move onto something you're an expert at."

"Talking," I said. "I'm quite adept at **say it**. I'm claiming those empowering words."

Unexpected laughter bubbled up and I held my hand over my mouth until it subsided.

"Care to let me in on what's so funny?" George asked.

"I was thinking of the last level, **do it**. I'll never forget how nervous you were during the tram ride up to the top of Squaw Valley."

George flashed a grin. "Some things are meant to be done only once in a lifetime and I sure hope that's one of them."

The waiter appeared, cleared the plates, and returned with the dessert menu. George smiled when he saw the house special, apple strudel. "I'll have the apple strudel with vanilla ice cream." He illustrated by placing one palm atop the other.

Although my mouth was watering for a slice of strudel, I passed.

While George savored his dessert, he continued, "Let's talk more about the affirmations. How did you think you did?'

"I've gone over them again and again and I have to admit, several come naturally and others I struggle with. It's rather like climbing a mountain and believing when I get to the top everything will be easier. It seems I never stay on top. Sometimes I slide back down, you know, like an avalanche."

"Think of it this way. You're stepping back a little to see the larger picture so you can move forward with better understanding and stronger conviction. I believe it was Einstein who said, 'The same mind that created the problem cannot solve it.' Your higher consciousness anticipates your questions. When you ask, expect the answer, then listen carefully for the answer and never doubt it. That's your intuition guiding you."

"You're so intent on me getting this intuition stuff, I feel like you're tutoring me for a final exam," I said.

"Donna, you'll understand someday that by trusting your intuition you'll have the ability to master your destiny."

"That is a little intense."

As we were leaving the restaurant, George glanced toward the water. "I'm ready for a good smoke. Let's go talk to those rollicking sea lions."

Once settled down on a bench, George went through his pipe-lighting ritual, puffing until he was satisfied with his handiwork. Cherry-scented smoke permeated the air. After three or four minutes of watching the frolicking sea creatures, I saw some of them turn their heads towards George and stare.

There was a current of communication between George and the sea lions. His unspoken dialogue with them was uncanny. Every few seconds, he would nod his head at the creatures and a few would flap their flippers and nod in return. A few of the pups let out their trademark barking sounds. I was mesmerized by the scene playing out before me and understood it was a living example of what George would refer to as silent communication or telepathy.

It was the same type of thought transfer that had occurred with the man who wanted to take his life when we were crawdad fishing. "George, you're connecting with the sea lions, aren't you?"

He leaned forward a little, drawing on his pipe. "They love to socialize. They have a pretty good life here." George peered over his glasses. "You connect like this with your cat. Most of us do it subconsciously. Everyone has the ability to communicate with animals. The secret is to take the time to develop the talent and send out positive vibrations. I am telling these big buddies how exquisite they are. Yep, mighty fine creatures, I must admit. Glad they are here on the earth."

I opened my mouth and closed it again when George put up his hand, admonishing, "I'm not saying it's easy," as he leaned back against the bench. "I know I've said this dozens of times, but I'll say it again: keep up with your meditation. You can have telepathic communication with animals and people as well. Now that I have your full attention, let me go on."

I nodded, staring at him.

"Certain things happen simultaneously that you might call coincidence but they aren't. They're manifestations of the Universe answering your prayers. You will receive help unexpectedly and from sources you didn't anticipate." George continued, "Most people aren't aware of the opportunities that await them if they would only stop talking and quiet themselves long enough to listen for the answers. That's why I keep drilling meditation into you. It's the stuff of miracles. It's how I achieved my knowing."

"Yes, I remember you telling me how your father had you meditate every morning, even before the roosters crowed."

He nodded and continued, "I dreaded waking up that early, but my father was wise beyond his years. He helped me develop my intuition at an early age. The seventh son of a seventh son."

"I have it—meditate, meditate, meditate. What else do I need to do?"

"There's something I call total release. You might call it forgiveness, or getting rid of baggage. It's the practice of letting go of things that anger or upset you. Whatever creates negative energy in your life, you have to let go. At the end of each day, before you put your head on the pillow, release the stress and think about the last time you felt true joy. Rekindle that feeling in your heart and mind. Recall how you felt gratified when your precious Sheba was curled up in your lap, purring away. Total release is a technique for grounding yourself and staying healthy. It keeps your energy aligned," George insisted.

"You're getting ahead of me," I admonished.

"Sorry, Partner, it's the engineering background in me coming out. Let me start again. Here's an example: if there are people you don't like, and you harbor ill will toward them but you act outwardly pleasant, they still get the sense of your true feelings."

"Even if I don't confess that to anyone? They still know it?"

"Yes. Whoever receives that energy can send bad energy back to you three-fold."

"Whew!" I exclaimed, "the first thing I have to do is stop sending out negative vibes. Do you have any suggestions on how I can protect myself when I have that bad energy coming my way?"

"When you feel threatened, you can ask for protection from the Universe. Close your eyes and imagine you are surrounded by a protective white light. Then if negative energy comes your way, the white light will deflect it. It sounds simple, but you must ask for protection and then believe with all your spirit that you are protected by the light."

"That was how I felt in the plane crash. Protected! How often can I put this white light around me?" I asked, giving George's arm an excited squeeze.

"Well, let's hope it's not the sort of thing you'll need to do every day, but when you're threatened or feel the need to protect yourself, trust your intuition and ask for protection."

"Mr. Mentor Man, there is something I want to ask you. During many nights after the plane crash, I'd wake up and sense a positive energy—not negative, but a loving presence of someone in the room, except no one was there. Was that my imagination?"

George narrowed his eyes. "During the crash you asked to live and change your life. What you felt those nights was the energy of spirits helping to heal you. These spirits, guardian angels, divine guides, or whatever you call them, are serving to help awaken your spirituality. Their assignment is to guide you to enlightenment. What you felt was their pure, loving energy."

"But where do these spirits come from?"

"That's difficult to describe exactly, but simply put, nothing ever completely dies. When the body succumbs, the soul takes on a different energy form. When I pass on, I already know that my time with you won't be over. I'll still be guiding you. Heaven help me, there is no rest."

I didn't like where this was headed and blurted out, "George, I don't want to even think about that. There's still so much I don't understand. How will I continue to learn without you here to help me?"

"Someday you will be a mentor."

My head buzzed with the implications of what he'd explained. "Maybe I'll smell your pipe. Do they let you smoke a pipe on the other side?"

George smiled. "I certainly hope so."

"Did I smell your pipe tobacco when I was in Marin visiting my friends, Brad and Isa? That was you, wasn't it?"

"Yes, that was me."

"How do you do that?"

"I am not going into all the details now, but always, and I mean always, trust your intuition. You knew it was me. Even if it doesn't make sense rationally, your intuition is wiser than your brain. I was visiting via another level when you were with your friends. By the way, mighty fine people. Sure have lots of love between them." He had that faraway look in his eyes as if he understood something of importance. "Intuition is perceived in a fleeting moment or a sudden feeling. Often these brief encounters are gone in an instant. Do you recall the messages you received during the plane crash?"

"Yes! I'll never forget them!"

Do you love yourself?
Do you have a good relationship
with your family and friends?
Are you living your goals and dreams?
If you die today, have you left this planet
a better place for being here?

"Each of those questions speaks to issues you have in your life—learning lessons, if you will. Donna, there are no accidents. You were in the plane crash so you could alter your thinking by looking at life a different way. Do you know how each one of these assignments affects your spiritual growth?"

"I answered no to each of those questions during the crash. My goal now is to answer yes. Do I love myself? That's work in progress, but I'm much better at it than I used to be. Every day I thank God I am alive."

I was quiet for some time. "As far as my relationships with family and friends go, I can answer yes to half of that question. My friends are great, but I yearn to heal with my father, mother, and brother."

He looked directly at me. "You will heal with each of them. Don't give up; keep working at it and believing. Listen to me when I say you will heal with each one of them. I promise you will. All right, let's move on. Are you living your goals and dreams?"

"I'm pleased with the goals I've achieved. Leaving Los Angeles, buying a home in Lake Tahoe, and starting my own business. Those are major accomplishments that I tend to overlook sometimes. I've grown more secure in my life. I'd still love to get married, but if that's not in the cards, my real dream is to have a daughter."

"Your cat is training you to be a mom, and doing an outstanding job. I understand how you long to have a family. Donna, know that a daughter is waiting to enter your world and will bring plenty of love into your life. She's coming sooner than you think. She's a pistol, but don't worry, I'll be right there by your side smoking my pipe. I wouldn't miss the big event for anything."

"Oh, that sounds wonderful."

"There is also the part about helping people help themselves."

"I'm working on helping people through my speeches, but I can't help but feel it's the blind leading the blind."

"One step at a time. We teach what we need to learn. Not to worry; the answers you seek will be revealed to you. For now, always know that I love you, believe in you, and will be around to guide you."

"Are you okay, George?"

"I'm fine, Partner." Slowly, George continued, "Focus on your intuition to contact me."

"George, please tell me that you're not leaving me today."

"No, not today, not today."

I felt compelled to say something. "George, I have always given you a hard time. Maybe it's the Irish in me or my stubborn streak, whatever. You have believed in me and given me inspiration. I couldn't have come this far without you. I love you for that. Plus, I've called you all kinds of names from Mr. Miracle Worker to Mr. Wise Man and oh, those Georgeisms—I rolled my eyes dozens of time. Sorry. I trust you more than anyone else. You've told me I would have three major life lessons. The plane crash was one, I know that. My question is, how will I comprehend if it is a major lesson like you said, or just a lesson?"

He chuckled. "Without a doubt you will know when it is your turning point. That sounds a bit dramatic, but you will understand." George became quiet and had that look in his eyes. "You are a tough assignment. It took a few miracles to get you where you are today." Very softly he continued, "You have a few more on the way."

Journal
The Truth Beyond

Completed the 30 days of insights, so I am ready to be hit with a lightning bolt of success and happiness. Why doesn't it work that way? Easy doesn't always mean it is good, or hard doesn't always mean it is bad. Simple sentence, but deep, deep, deep. What I'm now understanding is that my life is like school: I'm always learning.

George is a powerful current in my life. His persistence and his outlook have altered how I perceive my place on this earth. Like he says, the goal is to get out of your own way, and LIVE IN THE MOMENT. Tall order! The good news is the gift of intuition gives me direction. My areas to improve in are balance, meditation, love, and life. Plus, stay out of the drama. Oh yes, earn some cash while I am at it.

Universe, thank you for the blessings in this lifetime. I choose to know in my heart that what happens is for a reason. At the end of each day, before I go to sleep, I promise to release stress and think about joy and love.

Smile more
Laugh more
Love more

Chapter Fourteen
Where Are You?

Love knows no boundaries

"Come on, open. Come on, open now." My hand fumbled with the key to my front door as my briefcase slid down my shoulder to my elbow. The door burst open and I tripped over my suitcase as I dashed into the house and grabbed the phone.

"Hello, this is Donna."

"Hi Donna, it's Jeanne, George's friend from Denver."

Of course I knew Jeanne, but her voice sounded different, strained. I had met her many times when I was in Colorado. George had informed me that he had been assigned ten men and two women to watch over. Jeanne was the other female. He always told me that I was the hardest assignment because my life was all over the place. I sensed there was some truth behind his statement.

My briefcase slid off my arm to the floor as I dropped my keys on the counter. "Jeanne, how are you?"

Her voice cracked. "Donna," she said softly, "I have something to tell you."

My gut tightened. The tone of her voice indicated that something was very wrong.

"George crossed over today," she said, choking back tears.

"No, no, no!" I gasped. "I talked to him last week. He was fine. He was in Dallas."

"He did cross over, Donna."

I kept turning Jeanne's words over in my mind. *Crossed over. George crossed over? He can't be gone. It couldn't be.* My throat tightened. "I can't believe it ... how ...?"

"It was sudden," she explained, her voice so low I could barely understand her. "He became ill in Texas. The doctor admitted him into the hospital. He was diagnosed with cancer, and gone within a few days."

"I can't believe he's gone ... so quickly. Please, I hope he didn't suffer. Jeanne, how will we live without him?"

"You know he said he'll always be here for us, but in a different way. I have to go; we'll talk more later." Her voice trailed off and I heard the soft click of a disconnect. Fighting back tears, I hung up and began pacing around the room.

George would say I was wearing a hole in the carpet as I walked the same circle over and over again. Talking to myself, my eyes drifted toward the ceiling. "It can't be. It just can't be. You said you would be here for me. I don't believe it. Why didn't you tell me? Oh no, maybe you tried to tell me when we were in San Francisco. I was so concerned about my problems I wasn't truly listening to what you were telling me. That's why I felt you were prepping me for a final test. You were so intense. You wanted to make sure I understood about intuition." Tears rolled down my cheek.

"Are you all right, George? Where are you? Your body is still here on earth, but where did your spirit go? Are you in pain? Do you feel anything? Can you see me? Are you here? Can you check in on your family? Will they know you are with them?"

I could imagine George saying, "Slow down, you are accelerating. I can't answer that many questions at one time." Eventually, I quit pacing and flopped down on the sofa. I adjusted my body, uncrossed my legs, and closed my eyes to evoke memories of George. I pictured him in his pinstripe shirt and a navy blue blazer, his thinning brown hair with wisps of gray on the sides of his keenly intelligent face. He had his blooming pipe hanging from the left side of his mouth, and the aroma of cherry tobacco filled the air.

"George, are you listening?" I asked. I opened my eyes and stared at the ceiling. "I was blessed the day I met you. Talk to me, George. I feel so alone, so sad. Give me a sign." I pleaded, "Let me know you are all right."

I tried to meditate but nothing happened. I had difficulty focusing. Still no George. Perhaps he wasn't where he was meant to be yet, I rationalized. It must take time to make the journey to the other side. I should wait awhile and try again.

I couldn't wait. I started pacing again, then stopped cold.

You can't contact me in traditional ways, but even if you can't see me, Partner, I am with you in spirit. I'm your guardian angel.

I gasped, "George!"

 # Journal
Where Are You?

George, oh George, I love you. I never said thank you enough, so I'm saying it now. I know the words sound so trite, but I mean it. Why did I never think you'd be gone? I took it for granted you would be here.

I'm going to practice the lessons you've passed on to me, but if I falter, and I will, would you mind showing up and giving me a little guidance? Okay, let me change that—a lot of guidance. You said all I had to do was ask and then you could intervene and guide me. You also were adamant that if I didn't ask for assistance you couldn't step in and help me. You told me that many times when I received intuitive feelings, I was being guided from the other side. Now I understand why you were pushing me to develop my intuition. So if you think you are going to rest, wherever you are, think again. I still have many more questions that need answering. You are a blessing in my life.

You are my wise man
my mentor
and now my angel

Chapter Fifteen

Risk it All

Focus on what you want
Make it happen

Loss is devastating. Not only was I struggling to cope with the loss of George, but David, my wonderful friend from Los Angeles, had succumbed to HIV. Also, my surfing buddy Clayton had died of a sudden heart attack in Hawaii. The only blessing was that my friend Brad with MS seemed to have a reprieve.

Several times during the year that George passed, I'd reach for the phone to call him, but he was no longer there. I buried myself in my work, but my heart wasn't in it. Everything seemed to be crashing down around me. I had become manic about asking for a sign from George. I felt alone and unsure of how I would continue. Meditation was non-existent; I couldn't focus.

"George, please send me a message."

Feeling empty, I sat on the floor. I must have fallen asleep at some point, and awoke feeling numb. In my silent stupor an image started to formulate in my mind. At first I couldn't make out what it was, but then the image became more vivid. I massaged my temples as the characteristics of an infant with brown hair came into view. The child was wrapped in a pink blanket. "Mommy, I'm coming soon. Mommy, it's me. Mar ... Mar ... Mariah." June, I sensed the end of May or yes, the month of June somehow. Was she going to arrive before my birthday on July 1?

Bolting upright, I whispered, "Mariah, Mariah, your name is Mariah. When? When are you coming?" The room was still. I sensed nothing. George and I had talked about my daughter so often; I knew his spirit was somehow guiding the vision. My wise sage was telling me to get on with my life. I had a job to do. Raise a daughter. Be prepared. If I was sitting across from him having breakfast, he would insist I get off my butt.

Acting on my intuition, it was time to risk it all. I took out a line of credit on my house to pay the adoption agency in full. That was nerve-racking. Next, I did my home study, went shopping, and busied myself putting the final touches on my daughter's nursery. Mariah. That was her name. I loved that name. Then the name Chelsea popped into my head. That would be her middle name. It's where I had known her soul before, in England. She had been my daughter. *What? What?* My head dropped into my hands. *What am I thinking? Am I losing it or is my intuition telling me the truth?*

After paying the adoption agency, I waited and then waited some more. Other birth mothers had rejected me in the past, so I was afraid the same scenario was going to play out again. In May, the adoption agency called with the name of an expectant couple from Reno, Nevada, who had selected me as a prospective parent for their baby. I was thrilled beyond words. I was chosen and I would be a mom. Driving to Reno to meet the couple, I had difficulty staying within the speed limit. The mother-to-be was radiant and very quiet. The father was the one in charge. I liked them, but more importantly they seemed to think I would be a great parent for their child. The agency called a few days later, after the mother had a sonogram, to tell me the baby was a boy.

A flood of thoughts raced through my mind. The baby was a boy. How could that be? I had always envisioned a girl. Something was wrong. I didn't feel this child was right for me. The agency sensed my hesitancy and cautioned that I might not have another opportunity because I was an older, single applicant. They said they didn't know when, or if, there would be another infant for me.

That night I prayed for guidance, asking if I was the right mother for this boy. "What is his destiny?" I pleaded. I asked again and again and then waited. Then I sensed something. He would be a quiet child with a talent for computers. Being an over-the-top drama queen and slightly challenged on the computer, my brain kept insisting I couldn't help this child fulfill his dreams.

The next morning with my hands shaking, I dialed the birth parents' number. Softly, I said to the father, "I don't think I can be the mother for your son. Do you have anyone else in mind?"

"Yes," the father replied.

"What are they like?" I asked.

"They're rather quiet, and they run a computer business from their home," he simply stated.

"They'll be the perfect parents for your little boy. I'm honored that I was the first choice to raise your child, but I realized that I'm not the right person to help fulfill your son's future. He belongs with the other couple."

When the agency learned that I had declined the baby boy, they were livid; actually, "livid" was an understatement. I held the phone far from my ear and yet I could still hear the lady from the agency yelling. I had blown the chance to adopt an infant. I was in my mid forties and single, she reminded me sharply. Add it up; the opportunity wouldn't arise again. I knew my name was going to the bottom of the list or, worse yet, in the garbage bin.

Calmly I replied, "A daughter will come to me soon. Her name is Mariah and she will be born between May 20 and July 5 of this year." Strangely, the words just came out of my mouth. I was certain of the dates.

"Good luck." I heard *click*, and then a dial tone.

That night I went to bed resolved that I had done the right thing. Not so in the morning. My mind plagued me with doubts. My decision had been too hasty. I should have given it more thought. The agency had done their part and found me a healthy child and I was the one being stubborn. George's words echoed in my mind: *Follow your intuition; it will guide you.*

Nine days later the adoption agency called. In a very formal voice the woman said, "We have expectant birth parents in Las Vegas, and they have selected you to be the adoptive mother for their baby girl. She is due to arrive in six weeks near the end of June. Donna, this is a rare opportunity; they had your bio and personal information for over a month before they made a decision. This almost never happens," she insisted.

Softly I said, "A dear friend of mine told me to always trust my intuition. Yes, this is my daughter, I know it."

After I was given permission to contact the birth parents, I rehearsed what I would say, even practicing on my cat. I picked up the phone, put it down, made a sandwich, took two bites, and then rehearsed with my cat again. I practiced dialing their number twice more before actually making the call.

"Hello, Kelly, this is Donna Hartley. The adoption agency said I should call."

"Umph."

"Yes, I see. I've, well ... I know you have chosen me to be the mother of your ... daughter. I ... I don't know what to say, except that I'm so thankful." To say that the conversation was strained would be a huge understatement. I kept chattering away to fill in the uncomfortable lulls in the conversation. I had so many questions, but held back from asking many of them, not wanting to overwhelm the birth mother during our first chat. I needed her to like me. I learned Kelly was divorced and had a son from her first marriage. Later, Kelly and Conner, the birth father of this child, had a daughter together who was now three years old.

Kelly's pregnancy was not planned, and in fact they had been off and on for awhile and now separated, and Conner was seeing another woman. To make matters more complicated, Conner had a child with the girlfriend he was with now. Kelly couldn't possibly support another child on her own and Conner had recently lost his job. Under the circumstances, they both agreed it was best to place the baby up for adoption.

Kelly explained, "I want to let you know that both Conner and I independently picked you as first choice. We had six prospective parents, and after looking over the paperwork and your bio, I chose you first. Then Conner took the paperwork and studied it in another room and he chose you first. All the others were couples, but there was something about you that stood out."

During our next phone chat, I agreed to fly Kelly and Conner to San Francisco to meet with the agency. Afterward, I would drive them to my home in Lake Tahoe, take them to dinner, and then fly them back to Las Vegas the next day. They both liked the idea and would bring their daughter Amanda with them, but Kelly's son would stay with his grandparents.

On the day they were due to arrive in San Francisco, I showed up at the airport early, and commenced pacing back and forth while wondering if my flowered skirt and jersey top were appropriate attire. I eagerly scanned each exiting passenger, scoping for a pregnant woman. I anguished whether to hug them, shake hands, or just wave. As the arrivals thinned out to a few stragglers, I gave up hope, when suddenly three of them appeared at the gate.

Approaching them slack-jawed, I tentatively reached out a hand and said, "Welcome."

Kelly said demurely, "Sorry. I was so nervous about meeting you that I held back from exiting the plane."

Nodding my head I said, "Of course, I know what you mean."

Noticing her little daughter, I bent down and asked, "You're Amanda, right? Guess what?" I scooped a floppy-eared friend out of my tote bag and said, "This stuffed bunny insisted on coming along to meet you. Will you take care of him and be his friend?"

She smiled shyly and hugged it to her chest. She looked at her mother, then back at me. "Thank you," Amanda said in a sweet voice.

Kelly looked like a typical expectant mother, tired but radiant. She wore her lustrous brown hair pulled back in a ponytail. Conner was slim, over six feet tall, and had thick, dark hair with a slight cast of red. He carried their only suitcase.

"We'll be going to the agency first, about forty-five minutes away from here, and I can point out landmarks along the way to Walnut Creek if you like."

"That'll be great," Conner stated. "We've never been to San Francisco before."

We had separate sessions with the counselor at the agency. There were reams of paperwork for Kelly and Conner to read and sign, allowing time for Amanda and me to read books, play blocks, and color. She was a sweet, outgoing child. Every time the office door opened, I jumped. As time passed, my tension mounted as I obsessed about what was being said and whether they had changed their minds.

I was the last one to meet with the adoption counselor. I had a barrage of nonstop questions: "Do they like me? What did the medical reports show? Is the child healthy? Can they change their minds at the last minute?"

In a noncommittal tone, she said, "Everything is okay and on schedule."

My inner voice was intoning, *Stay calm, relax; it will work out.* My irrational mind was harping, *Are you nuts? It's not done, anything can happen.*

During the drive to Lake Tahoe, we had hours to talk. Amanda and Kelly fell asleep while Conner and I discussed our English-Irish backgrounds, favorite books, movies, and the importance of school. Relaxed in his mannerisms, Conner was easy to talk to. At 27, he felt that he had missed out on a fulfilling career by not attending college. He hadn't been guided in that direction by his family, and was adamant that his child have the opportunity for a good education in high school and a college degree. I made a promise to him that I would fulfill his wish.

"Oh my gosh, it's beautiful," Kelly exclaimed, awakening from her nap. "I've never seen mountains this magnificent before. The lake is ... it's ... breathtaking."

This was a far cry from Las Vegas. Her eyes widened as we pulled into the driveway of my home. When she walked into Mariah's nursery, done in animal décor, she ran her hands over the baby books, sat back in the pastel rocking chair, and sighed, "I could stay here forever."

Conner, on the other hand, checked out the books on my shelves. "So where did you graduate from college?"

"University of Hawaii. Loved the college life. When I wasn't studying I was out surfing."

"I'm sorry I missed out on the whole college experience, but I did excel in math in high school."

"Then I hope your daughter has strong math genes because I can't help her in that area," I stated.

After dinner, Kelly put her energetic daughter to bed in Mariah's nursery and Conner turned toward the guest room, wearily saying, "Good night."

Propped up in bed with the light on, I replayed the day's events in my mind.

A while later, as Kelly was returning from the bathroom, she paused at my bedroom door. "Can I come in and talk?" she asked tentatively.

"Sure."

She sat down on the edge of the bed and hugged a pillow to her pregnant tummy. "Donna, I read your bio and the answers on the agency questionnaire, but meeting you in person has really eased my mind. I've worried so much about the baby's well-being. Now that we've met, I'm sure I made the right decision. Actually, you're more like an aunt to me than someone I hardly knew until today. See, I was raised by my grandparents and I'm real close to my Aunt Pat."

Her eyes grew large as she glanced around the room. "Your house is homey. The lake, the mountains, the small-town atmosphere—it's a great place for a child to grow up. We could never give her this."

Kelly squeezed the pillow tighter. "Could I ask you a favor? You don't have to say yes, but would you send a picture or two?"

"I wouldn't mind at all," I replied. "What if I send pictures on her birthday and at Christmas?" Kelly seemed pleased. This time I was the one who fiddled with a pillow. For my peace of mind, I felt it necessary to clarify some adoption ground rules.

"Kelly, now I have a favor to ask of you and Conner."

"Okay," she replied.

"Until the baby is born, she's yours and you have the right to change your mind about the adoption. By Nevada law you have seventy-two hours after she's born. Once you sign the papers, she becomes my daughter. I would like to tell her about you. How do you feel about that, Kelly?" No oxygen entered my lungs as I waited for her response.

At first she said nothing. The silence was nerve-racking. "I guess I feel okay. I think you're meant to be her mother. I ... I already have a son and a daughter. I'm not married and don't have the money to raise another child. I work in a casino and Conner has been unemployed for months. Now he's living with another woman."

She gazed at me intently before continuing. "We want to know the baby will be loved and raised in a nice home, and that she'll have a better life than we could offer. Education is really important, especially to Conner. Security is a major concern of mine."

"Thank you, Kelly, for believing in me. I will love her," I said. "I'm going to name her Mariah."

"Yeah. That's really cool. I like the name Mariah," Kelly said, easing herself up from the bed. "I like it a lot." As she made her way toward the door she paused a moment and said, "Thanks, Donna, and good night."

The next day, after Kelly, Conner, and Amanda boarded their flight back to Las Vegas, I sat motionless in the car for a long time. After all the years of waiting, was this really happening? It seemed like it was.

The next step was to call all my girlfriends, who wanted to throw me a baby shower. I was beyond excited when I told them about the birth parents and the due date for the baby in June, even remaining enthusiastic when a few of them asked, "What if the birth mother changes her mind?"

Relying on my resolve, I cast their doubts aside. I couldn't even think about that happening. My focus was on moving ahead and planning for the future. If George were here I knew he would insist I act on my intuition. He was a stickler about visualizing results. The end result for me was that I had my daughter.

Over the next few weeks, I completed stacks of adoption papers. Just when I thought I'd filled everything out, another pile would arrive in the mail.

Inspecting Mariah's room for the hundredth time, I made sure everything was ready and perfect, right down to the fluffy pink blankets and disposable diapers. The animal theme was accented with a big, colorful fabric palm tree. I even cooked two weeks' worth of meals and stored them in the freezer.

I was ready. The doctor had scheduled Kelly's Cesarean for June 23rd. I would fly out the day before. My anticipation was so exhilarating that I couldn't fall asleep at night. My girlfriends kept lecturing me to sleep now, while I still could. It was 6:30 PM on June 20th when the phone rang. An unfamiliar woman's voice said, "Hi, Donna, I'm Kelly's friend Nan. You are the proud mother of a healthy, beautiful, nine-pound four-ounce baby girl. She's 21 inches long and was born at 6:06 this evening."

In spite of all my planning and sleepless nights, Mariah had decided to enter the world in her own time. I recalled George saying, "She's gonna be an independent little thing," and wondered if this was a sign of things to come.

"Are you sure the baby is okay?"

"Fine, and very healthy," she assured me.

Questions raced through my mind. "Is Kelly doing well? Were there complications?"

"No complications," Nan replied, "They are both doing great. Kelly told me that right after she talked to you this afternoon, her water broke and they rushed her straight to the hospital."

I was hanging on every word. "Tell Kelly I'll be on the first morning flight to Las Vegas. What's the name of the hospital?"

"Sunrise Hospital," Nan replied.

Pack, pack, I had to pack. I rushed around the house like a woman possessed, pulling out a suitcase and carry-on bags, dashing from room to room gathering diapers, plastic bottles, formula, toothbrush, and baby clothes. Oh, and the baby car seat, too.

I didn't take time to think how I would get it all on the plane. My mind kept checking off items and I kept tossing them into the bags.

Suddenly, reality hit. The magnitude of Kelly giving birth had my nerves jumping like hot sparks. I plopped down on the floor amidst all the clutter and reflected. Seventeen years ago, in the midst of a plane crash and entombed in a burning inferno, I heard a voice say that I would speak, write, and have a daughter. Finally my answer to that was, "Yes, yes, and yes!" This was it! I was actually going to be a mom!

The thought of calling my mother in Pennsylvania to give her the news made me apprehensive. Every time I broached the subject of adoption, she had insisted that it was a crazy idea, and that if I continued to pursue it she would write me out of her will. Come on, a baby—how could she not want a grandchild? My mother had a good heart, so I knew she would understand.

I dialed the number and waited. Excitedly, I said, "Mom, a baby girl was born in Las Vegas tonight, and she is healthy. I'm flying there tomorrow morning."

"Donna, you are too old to adopt a baby."

"Mom, I'm not too old. I'm forty-seven."

"And in ten days you're going to be forty-eight."

"So."

"Now you'll never get a man. It takes time and money to raise a child on your own and you don't have either. You could lose your house." She hung up.

"Mom ... Mom ..." I stood there staring at the receiver. Her crushing words punched the air right out of me. Why couldn't she be happy for me? She was Mariah's grandmother. My child would be her only grandchild. I yearned for someone to be happy for me.

Next, I dialed my brother. Having never wanted children of his own, he seemed barely lukewarm about the news. "Donna, are you sure this is the right move for you?"

"Yes I am."

"Then good luck, but I don't think this is the best thing for you."

By the time I called my father in Nevada, I felt empty and ready for any reaction.

"I'm flying to Las Vegas first thing tomorrow morning to adopt my daughter."

He didn't hang up, and actually seemed pretty excited about the news.

"Have a safe trip and when you get home, please call me. I would like to come over and see your daughter. What's her name?"

"Her name is Mariah and her middle name is Chelsea."

"Great. I look forward to meeting her."

I was somewhat surprised by my father's reaction.

Feeling more confident, I dialed my stepdad's number at work. I always considered John to be my daddy. John always accepted me for who I was. He was kind and patient. A great listener, he ran a bar and listened to all—the wins, losses, lies, and excuses, and sometimes even the truth came with the territory. He was a good judge of character.

"I'm going to Las Vegas to adopt my daughter, but when I told Mom she hung up on me."

"Don't worry," he said. "Your mother will come around. She wants the best for you. She's remembering how tough it was to raise you and your brother by herself." Then he gave me a real boost by saying, "You've always wanted a family. I think it's wonderful. It's your life. Don't let anyone steal your dream."

"Thank you, Daddy. I won't." Our relationship had convinced me that love, not blood, makes a family. Mariah wouldn't be my biological child, but she would be loved by me.

At Sunrise Hospital, I scanned the room numbers in the maternity ward and finally located Kelly. She was sitting up while holding the baby, the perfect mother and daughter picture. My heart had an extra flutter. *Please tell me this is going to be my daughter.* For years I had dreamed of this moment. Kelly handed me the child. I took her in my arms and gazed down at the tiny, perfect baby with waving arms and tight-clenched fists. I held her like a fragile china doll, so overwhelmed with emotions I couldn't move.

"Relax. She's not going to break," Kelly said.

I chuckled. "That obvious?"

When Mariah let out a wail, my motherly instincts came alive and I cooed and rocked her as if it were an everyday occurrence. The diaper event proved to be more difficult. Kelly laughed at my clumsiness while changing Mariah. Her tiny body seemed lost in the huge diaper.

"How many diapers have you changed?" Kelly asked, eyeing my bumbling efforts.

"None," I replied, "but I'm a fast learner."

Custody of a child is granted to the birth parents for seventy-two hours in Nevada. Within that time period, they can decide to keep the child or place the infant up for adoption. The social worker was adamant: I could not have physical contact with the baby unless Kelly was present to hand the child to me. I made a point to follow the rules, but I spent every moment possible in the hospital room with Kelly and the newborn.

Kelly was alone with Mariah from 7:00 AM until public visiting time at 11:00 AM I was keenly aware that Kelly had those four hours every morning to bond with the baby. I worried that she might change her mind about giving up Mariah—a lingering fear relieved only when I cradled my daughter in my arms.

Every evening when visiting hours were over, I returned the baby to Kelly, and the cold knot of uncertainty reappeared. Aside from my apprehensions about the birth mother changing her mind, I felt troubled over Conner's feelings about the adoption. At the hospital he remained a shadowy presence in the background.

My opportunity to talk to him came while we were standing at the nursery window peering in at the babies and watching Mariah sleep peacefully in her bassinet.

"It's a blessing Mariah is so beautiful and in such good health," I remarked.

"Yes," Conner said, and then he was quiet. There was awkwardness between us.

He turned to me. "You'll give her direction. She needs a good education." There was not a speck of regret on his face. "I will make that happen."

As we walked away from the nursery, he paused and studied me for a moment. "You know, she was never meant to be my daughter. Do you think it's weird how two strangers gave you what you wanted more than anything in the world?"

"Weird? Maybe not so weird but more like destiny. I love her."

His education might have been limited to high school, but he was very insightful.

At last the day had arrived for the adoption, and there were only a few hours left to wait. I called the state agency to confirm that my social worker would be at the hospital for the signing of the papers. I was told she was on vacation and I would have to wait until Monday.

"What, Monday? But it's Friday! I can't wait until Monday!"

"Sorry, but those are the rules. We'll confirm with the birth mother that she can either take the child home or we'll have the baby placed in foster care for the weekend."

"But ... that's not acceptable. The seventy-two hours are almost up. We have to sign the papers," I pleaded, panic mounting with every word. "Please, can't someone else help?"

"Call back in an hour. I'll see what I can do."

Sixty minutes seemed like sixty hours. I paced the hospital corridor, wringing my hands, eyeballing the clock, and praying for the minute hand to grow wings, angel wings.

I was so distraught that I couldn't bear to discuss the pending situation with Kelly. I only told her there were some details the agency had to work out. The moment the minute hand hit the hour, I dialed the number.

"We have good news," the woman confirmed. "We contacted your social worker at home. She's willing to come into the hospital for the signing."

Enormously relieved, I walked into Kelly's room to share the good news, but immediately saw how distressed she was. Conner had not been at the hospital all day. I assured her the social worker was on her way and would be at the hospital by 6:00 PM As it was only 4:40, we still had time.

"I sure hope he shows up," she said, sounding irritated.

However, when the social worker and the notary arrived, there was still no sign of Conner. Thanking them both for giving up their time, I was told it would take about two hours to get through the official paperwork. Kelly kept fidgeting and watching the clock.

By the time Conner arrived, it was obvious that Kelly was furious.

"Where were you?" she blurted out. "We need to talk."

The social worker glanced at Kelly, then Conner, and finally her eyes settled on me.

"Donna, will you please leave the room now?"

The door closed behind me as I leaned against the hospital corridor wall. I had been so sure this was going to work. I had taken out a second on my house. *Oh no, it's not going to happen. She's not going to be my daughter.* Slowly, my body slid down the wall until I collapsed on the cold floor.

Chapter Sixteen

The Mysterious Smoke

Center your energy
Trust the Universe will provide

When the social worker walked out of the hospital room, I sprang to my feet.

"It's settled," she said.

"Oh no," I screamed as I covered my face. With a muffled voice I blurted out, "My daughter ... but my—"

"No. This issue had nothing to do with you, Donna. They were fighting about Conner being late because he was with his girlfriend. We can proceed. You and Kelly can go to the nursery and bring the baby back here while I read Conner his birth-father rights."

"You mean everything's fine? It's not me? I can still adopt my daughter?"

"Yes," the social worker confirmed.

"You're sure?"

"Yes."

"Thank you so much," I sniffled, and then let out a huge sigh of relief.

Kelly (proceeding slowly due to her Cesarean) and I (walking on air) headed toward the nursery. I witnessed her signing Mariah out, and we wheeled the bassinet down the hallway.

As we paraded slowly toward her room, Kelly suddenly stopped. She lifted her head, turned it left, and sniffed in that direction. A sharp blade of fear knifed through me. There wasn't much time left, but she still had the right to change her mind. Clutching my stomach with one hand, I gripped the bassinet with the other to steady myself. What could be wrong now?

I cautiously asked, "Kelly, are you all right?"

She said nothing.

"We should move along."

I feared that Kelly might already have regrets. What if she changed her mind in these last few minutes? I felt a bond with the baby—my Mariah—so tiny in the bassinet, one little being engulfed in a world of pink blankets and the swirling desires of people around her. I giggled as her little fists punched the air. "A pistol," George had predicted. He was right; I'd be adopting a pistol of a child. If everything went well ... if Kelly signed.

"I smell smoke. No one is allowed to smoke in the nursery," Kelly complained as she darted into the room, seeking the source of the offensive odor.

Returning with a puzzled expression, she said, "I don't understand. No one is there, but I smell smoke. It smells like ... I don't know, maybe cherries."

Tears welled up in my eyes and my words caught in my throat. Focusing on Mariah, I struggled to speak. "George ... George promised he would be here when you came into my life ... he kept his promise. You are truly my daughter. George, are you listening? Of course you are." Struggling to continue I mouthed, "Thank you."

Sensing a bewildered stare from Kelly, I slowly shifted my gaze.

Her head was tilted and her mouth hung open.

"It's a long story, but the short version is that my friend passed away and I was heartbroken. He swore he'd be close by when I adopted my daughter. The aroma of cherry tobacco that permeated the air was his familiar scent. George, my mentor, smoked cherry tobacco in his pipe. I ... I don't know whether you believe in these things."

"But I smelled it first." She shook her head, bewildered. "I really don't believe in that stuff, but I can't deny the scent. How can that be?"

Scanning the hall as if expecting him to appear, I continued, "George taught me that life was eternal. He said he was assigned to watch over me."

"I need to tell you something," Kelly said rather ominously.

Please ... don't change your mind. "Sure," I said, scarcely able to look at her.

"Do you know why I chose you, a single woman in her forties, to raise my child?"

"No, I can't, I can only hope that ..." I sputtered, feeling my racing heart as nothing else would come out of my mouth.

Kelly looked down at Mariah, peacefully sleeping in the bassinet. "Don't ask me how, but I know this baby girl is going to do great things. I know you will help make it happen. I'm so busy working and raising Amanda and my son that I can't even think past the next day."

I confided to her, "During the plane crash, a voice spoke to me and said I would have a daughter late in life who would be a leader. George, my mentor, confirmed it."

Kelly glanced at the infant, then at me, and softly murmured, "Yes."

We wheeled the newborn into Kelly's room for the last milestone. Conner had carefully read through the documents. Holding Mariah in my arms helped to slow my heartbeat, but I was frazzled. Each time the social worker explained that Conner and Kelly had the right to change their minds before signing, my pulse raced. Why had I come here alone? I should have brought a girlfriend with me. What made me think I could do this by myself? Feeling overwhelmed, my breathing became shallow as I waited for the birth parents to finalize all the papers.

Two hours later, the grueling process was complete. Standing outside on the curb with Mariah in my arms, a flash of panic surfaced. Holding her closer to my chest seemed to help relieve my uncertainties.

"Here we go, sweetheart," I said gently.

She let out a whimper, and then yawned.

Placing Mariah gingerly on the motel bed, I removed her pink blanket. She was so tiny and beautiful. I held my pinkie close to her hand and she gripped it, as a new sensation tingled throughout my body. My night was a sleepless fiasco as I woke every hour to monitor her breathing and check her diaper. What if the formula disagreed with her? Would something awful happen if she didn't burp?

Early in the morning, I agonized over which outfit would keep the baby comfortable on our trip. I had brought way too much stuff. With Mariah in my arms, I made trip after trip to the elevator—car seat, suitcase, diaper carrier, and formula bag. When the doors of the elevator slid open, I used my foot to keep them from closing while clutching Mariah to my one free shoulder and stuffing our belongings inside.

When we reached the lobby, I pulled everything out of the elevator piece by piece, with my back propped against the door. Dragging the pile outside, I hailed a cab. I almost cried while tangling with the car seat. It wouldn't stay put. By the time I figured it out and strapped Mariah in, I was covered in sweat. The taxi driver sat there tapping his fingers.

The distance between the airport curb and the luggage check-in counter seemed like a mile. A father of two older children must have seen the panic on my face, and helped carry my luggage. An airline pilot finally stepped out behind the ticket counter to hold my daughter as I frantically rummaged through my purse for my ticket. Here I was, the mother of a four-day-old infant, completely overwhelmed with the complexity of travel.

Thinking we'd be more comfortable, I upgraded my ticket to first class for our flight home. I was elated until I saw the glares from the other passengers. Was there a rule that said not to bring a baby into first class? "Inconsiderate Person" must have been written on my forehead because even the flight attendant treated me like an outcast. My stress level rose as I realized that if Mariah cried we would be banished to some back corner. I prayed for a small miracle; she slept through the entire flight.

Upon landing, the woman seated across the aisle said, "Your baby was very good. I thought for sure she'd be fussy."

"Thank you. She's four days old and I'm so excited to bring her home. I've been trying to adopt for seven years, and I finally have my daughter."

The look on her face said it all. After that, she and her husband fell over themselves to help maneuver us through the airport.

Next, it took all my energy to place the baby car seat in the correct position in the back of my car, give Mariah a bottle, change her diaper, find my money, and get the car out of the airport parking lot. Was it just me, or did other new mothers feel this way—overwhelmed?

During the drive to Tahoe, my mind was whirling faster than a carnival ride. Could I take care of her when she got sick? Would I make her happy? How much should I set aside for her college fund? What if I got sick? Who would help? The questions piled up faster than I could answer them.

Crossing the threshold of my home, the enormity of what had

transpired registered in my mind. Tears rolled down my face in streams as my shoulders shook. Deliriously happy, I tried to take deep breaths to calm myself as the realization that years of pent-up hopes had become reality began to sink in.

Mariah's tiny body wiggled as I carefully placed her on my bed. Sheba's feline intuition had already told her that something monumental was about to take place. She hopped up, landing with a soft thud, and gently sniffed the baby. "Sheba, meet your sister Mariah."

Sheba stared at me, then at the baby, then back at me, until her brilliant blue eyes finally focused on Mariah. *This is what a sister looks like?*

Sheba pawed the corner of the pink blanket to straighten it out, then curled up at the bottom of the bed and went to sleep.

My friends had asked, "What if Sheba is jealous of the baby? What if the baby is allergic to the cat? What will you do?" I always thought to myself, *That won't happen. We will be a family.*

Gingerly placing Mariah in her bassinet I said, "Here sweetheart, go to sleep. Your mom and sister are going to take a nap, too."

Hallelujah! We are a family. Aren't we? It would take six more months for the adoption papers to be finalized in California, but I had a daughter. I was almost sure.

Journal
The Mysterious Smoke

Happiness ... love ... joy ... what words can describe what I'm feeling?

People had warned me about the work involved in raising a child, but hadn't informed me about the bonds of intimacy and love.

Dear George, you knew I'd be a mom. All those years I questioned you about when my daughter would arrive. She's really here, and she is gorgeous. Oh, her little toes are perfect, her pink fingernails, and her tummy is adorable. I could go on for hours about how lovable she is, and I know she is going to be smart.

I had serious doubts about you appearing at the adoption. Serious doubts. I know I can't pick up the phone and call you, yet ... the scent of your special blend of cherry pipe tobacco ... that was unmistakable. WOW. I am getting used to odd happenings as normal events. There is so much more to your spiritual teaching than I ever realized.

Thank you for confirming this baby as my daughter. Please ... and I mean please, stay close by. I know I'll be needing your help. Did you think you were going to rest on the other side? No way!

You're the seventh son of a seventh son and your wisdom is timeless. Master teacher, your reluctant student wants to make you proud. Keep an eye on me.

I miss you, George ...

Chapter Seventeen

You Know When You Know

Obstacles become valuable lessons
It's the lessons that move us forward
Trust your intuition

The Christmas season had officially arrived in Lake Tahoe. Crisp, unseasonably warm air whispered through the glistening pine forest. Snowcapped peaks floated on a cloudless skyline above the dazzling blue lake. I was enjoying a leisurely drive home after strolling Mariah through town to see the Christmas lights and stopping at the grocery store. My daughter was fast asleep in the back seat.

George had stressed the importance of balance, but raising an infant entailed sleepless nights and arranging my work schedule around bathing, napping, and feeding times. Many nights I wondered if every conscientious mother felt pulled in ten different directions.

When Mariah was three months old the unthinkable happened. I woke up and couldn't move my body. I couldn't even sit up. A girlfriend came to the rescue to take care of Mariah and then I called my father to drive me to the hospital in Truckee. The ER docs insisted there was nothing wrong with me that a week of sleep wouldn't cure. They called it "new mother syndrome."

I'd come a long way in the last six months, and now could easily juggle a purse and a diaper bag while holding the baby and her bottle. I'd cut my work schedule in half, for the time being. A new mom needs her sleep. I found out this "Wonder Woman" could not do it all.

Pulling into my driveway, I appreciated the welcome sight of my home bathed in winter sunlight. My Christmas tree dressed in crimson and silver glowed in the window. What made me smile the most was the thought that today the adoption papers had been finalized before the California judge. Mariah was officially my daughter. She was still snoozing in her car seat, and the number one rule I had learned was to let a sleeping kid sleep. I rolled the window down halfway so I could hear her as I unloaded the groceries.

Sheba, waiting at the door, gave me one of those looks that said, *Where's what's-her-name?* Placating her I said, "Your sister is in the car. I'm bringing in the groceries. Surprise, I brought you some yummy food."

A few minutes later, I opened the car door to get Mariah and was shocked to be greeted by the cat again.

"What are you doing here, Sheba? Did you jump in through the window?"

From her curled position next to Mariah, she seemed to say, *Somebody had to look after my sister. That's what I'm doing here.*

I had a family, maybe not the traditional kind, but I knew I had two little souls to take care of. I would never again question if love is enough. You know when you know.

Still laughing as I hoisted Mariah over one shoulder and Sheba over the other, I went inside and warmed a bottle, then sat down on the sofa to feed the baby. Sheba jumped up and nuzzled her nose on my lap. My decision to adopt had been a powerful one that had changed the course of our lives.

Laying Mariah down on her blanket, I saw her eyes widen as she was mesmerized by the Christmas tree lights. As I looked at my child, my cat, and the gifts under the tree waiting to be opened, the true meaning of Christmas flooded my mind: a time to give thanks to God, to recount all the lessons learned, and to plan for the new year. Mariah's first Christmas ... magical memories.

It saddened me to know that my mother and I wouldn't be sharing the holidays. Nonetheless, she had sent a check for Mariah and a box of gifts that had been sitting beneath the tree for weeks. Tenderly removing the wrappings, I found several darling baby outfits and a bunch of stuffed animals.

Clutching the yellow lion cub to my heart, I prayed that my mother's thoughtfulness was a sign she was accepting Mariah as her granddaughter. Was it so unreasonable of me to want to share a lifetime of Mariah moments as an infant, a toddler, and a young lady?

Gingerly, I dialed my childhood house phone number. It rang several times before my stepdad John answered.

"Hi, Daddy! I called to wish you and Mom a Merry Christmas."

"Back at you too, Donna. Merry Christmas. I'm afraid your mom's not home."

My body sagged with disappointment. "Okay, Daddy," I said, feeling the sting of tears. "Please thank her for the beautiful gifts she sent Mariah. The clothes are the perfect size and the animals are adorable. Would you please have her call me?"

"I'll give her your message, honey. How's the new mom? Getting any sleep yet?" he teased.

"Some. Never enough, Daddy, but I still love being a mom."

"I can hear it in your voice, Donna. Now, don't worry about your mother. I'm working on her and she'll come around. I think she's accepted Mariah. She has a problem with you being a single mom. She was a single mom for you and your brother and it wasn't easy. She remembers how difficult it was. But honey, you put that aside and have a wonderful first Christmas with your daughter."

"Thank you, Daddy. I love you."

I sat down and nodded off for a while. When the phone rang, I was so startled I almost knocked over the lamp reaching for it. "Hi, this is Donna."

"Hey, it's Jackie."

"Oh, hi, Jackie," I said wearily.

"Anything the matter? Is Mariah sick?" Jackie asked.

"No, we're fine. Sorry. I'm really glad to hear from you; thought you were my mother calling back."

We talked for a while, and after we hung up my reflections focused back on family and my brother. So much for blood; he hadn't even bothered to meet Mariah. She was already six months old and growing like a weed. Sure, as kids we had fought with each other, but we were always close. I guessed he was taking my mother's side regarding my being a single mom. It would be worth calling to wish him a Merry Christmas, and see if we could get together.

He answered on the third ring. "Doug! Hi, happy holidays. Are you coming up to Tahoe to ski anytime soon?"

"I might come up for New Year's."

"How about stopping by to meet Mariah? We'll be around, and she is adorable."

He paused a moment before answering, "I don't know ... might be busy with friends. Another time might work better."

Fighting disappointment, I cleared my throat. "Have a wonderful holiday anyway. See you soon."

Struck out two for two; not the best batting average.

At least my father had stopped by earlier—alone, not with my stepmother, but with a beautiful wooden highchair for Mariah. I was overwhelmed by his thoughtfulness and knew Mariah would be growing into it soon.

Snuggling up to Mariah I whispered, "It's you and me, kid. So here are the positive statements for the day. You are gorgeous. You are healthy. You are happy. You are talented. You are perfect." Sheba meowed as she moved closer. "Oh, I love you too. All right then, you want me to say positive things about you too. You are magnificent. You are regal. You have a blessed life." Sheba rolled over and stretched out her paws as if to say, *Yes this is all true. Is there anything more?* "Now, can I say positive affirmations about myself? I am healthy. I am a professional speaker. I have abundance. I love being a mom. I am blessed to have two daughters."

Glancing over at the mantel, I focused on George's picture and reminisced about the last day I saw him, when we strolled along Pier 39 in San Francisco. He had lectured me incessantly, and now I understood why. He was so insistent about meditating and trusting my intuition. I believe now he sensed he would be passing away within the year, yet he said nothing.

I'm sure he's up there looking down on me. Yeah, he's laughing at my fumbling and bumbling, plus my worrying about Mariah's hiccups, and my overly anxious calls to the pediatrician. "I'm doing it, George, and I'm learning what it means to be a mom." It didn't matter that he was nowhere to be seen. It felt good to be talking to my old friend.

"Mr. Wise Man, please give me your guidance. I was slow to understand your Georgeisms, but now I realize they were very enlightening messages. Yes, I'm a little impatient. Let me rephrase that, I am very impatient. This seems to be the time of year to tell you again how grateful I am for your being there for me. In case you don't know, you are my 'Number One Mentor.' Oh how I miss those early morning breakfasts, and even your blasted Georgeisms and the scent of your tobacco."

Finding myself in a melancholy mood I blabbered on, "Hey, George, will you continue to hear my SOS calls? I bugged you down here, so I might as well give you a hard time up there. Where is up there anyway? No rest for the weary. Your duty is not over yet. Here is my request. Healing with my family is a priority, and it seems that the path is blocked. Is there another way? I love them. Mariah needs grandparents and an uncle. Whether they know it or not, they need her."

My daughter watched me intently as I continued to talk. Even Sheba was fixated on me now. "Remember when I said that if I had a choice, I would never have chosen my parents, with their alcoholism and violence? You stood solid as old Ironsides and wouldn't budge on this issue, even though we discussed it year after year."

I got up and paced the room continuing, "George, your answer always stayed the same. Adamantly you would state, 'Donna, you chose your parents before you were born. They helped make you who you are by creating the lessons you were destined to experience. Thank them for the challenges. Now you will choose to alter the pattern in your family and raise your daughter with incredible love and laughter. You are the changing factor. Don't give up. You will heal with your family.'"

I crossed past the fireplace in the living room to the window. The night was clear and the starry sky shimmered. I'd come a long way since selling pots and pans to survive during my college days.

I glanced down at Mariah, kicking her little feet beneath the tree while cooing at the lights and shiny ornaments. So content. Except for the crackle of logs burning in the fireplace, the house was wrapped in silence. I looked up toward the sky. "I'm ready. I want to heal my life on all levels. I refused to pass on negative patterns to my daughter."

It was my little girl's first Christmas and celebration was on the agenda. Music would do the trick; a Christmas classic would be ideal.

Searching through my CDs, I found the Christmas music at the back of the shelf. An old copy of my *Is Your Attitude Showing?* workbook was wedged against the CDs. A small white envelope stuck out of the red workbook with "Donna" written in George's handwriting on it.

I had given him the workbook to review during a visit to Denver a couple of years back. When he returned it, his comment was, "This is a winner. Keep it in a safe place."

Quickly turning on the light, I tore open the envelope, finding a note from George and a poem.

Hi Partner —

When I came across this poem, I knew it would help you.

Do not stand at my grave and weep,
I am not there, I do not sleep.
I am a thousand winds that blow.
I am the diamond glints on snow.
I am the sunlight on ripened grain.
I am the gentle autumn's rain.
When you awaken in the morning's hush,
I am the swift, uplifting rush
of quiet birds in circled flight.
I am the soft stars that shine at night.
Do not stand at my grave and weep,
I am not there, I do not sleep.
Do not stand at my grave and cry.
I am not there, I did not die!

Mary Elizabeth Frye

Live your life. There is much for you to do. Get happy.
George

Tears rolled down my cheeks as I sat in the quiet room reading George's message again. I imagined his face, with a knowing smile lighting up his intense eyes, and pipe smoke curling around his head.

He was an ancient soul ... a man who practiced the truths of the ages and passed his wisdom on to me in very simple ways.

Keep it simple
Keep it truthful

Intuition is the simplest and most honest way to know what is right. Act on it.

You know when you know

My hand flew to my chest as an intuitive thought flashed through my mind. *You must heal with your family. You need to do it for your daughter's sake.* I answered the thought out loud. "How? How will I heal with my family? I want to, but ... where do I begin?"

I sat there in the silence waiting for something. A sign, anything, but nothing happened.

My fluffy cat slithered in next to Mariah, and kept batting at a sparkling silver ornament. Her actions pulled me from my quandary. Her playful demeanor was contagious, and I started to giggle.

"This has been some journey, you two. The unexpected has become the norm in our family. What next? We've got each other. Whatever happens, we'll make it."

Your Gift of Intuition

The gift of intuition is yours to claim. If you truly want to heighten your awareness:

- **Think It**

- **Feel It**

- **Visualize It**

- **Say It**

- **Do It**

Listed below are the 30 days of affirmations that George shared with me. I suggest you place this book on your nightstand or some place you will see it every day. Your goal is to develop your intuition by focusing on one affirmation each day. Claim these affirmations. You want to think, feel, visualize, say and do them as normally as you breathe in and out.

Notice the inner peace you will gain from doing this exercise. It takes some work and time, but never give up. You are worth it. These insights will alter your life, lift your energy, and advance your intuition. These affirmations are a road map to your inner knowing.

Let me end with a Georgeism. It took me years and years to understand, but now I truly know that the knowledge you seek is inside of you. When you slow down long enough to focus on the truth and access the knowledge, then you will know the answer that is right for you.

You know when you know

Day I

Attitude

You determine the outcome of each day when you wake up and your feet hit the floor. You decide whether it will be an intolerable day or a successful one, because 87% of success is attitude and 13% is skill.

Neither fame, fortune, nor beauty entitles you to a bad attitude. Improving your attitude is the first step toward changing your life. When your attitude centers on optimism, integrity, and managing your state, it empowers you.

Your attitude does NOT depend on the actions or behavior of other people. It's one thing that you totally create.

AFFIRMATION: I manage my attitude to create positive results.

Day 2

Confidence

Confidence is earned from learning the lessons you experience. It helps to define your actual purpose and it is supported by your values. It's the building block to success and the cement that keeps you from giving up. Like life, your confidence can experience highs and lows. Confidence is the belief in your own abilities to succeed. Only you can manage your confidence and no one has the right to take it away from you.

Listen to the voice inside you, trust your intuition and your feelings, and then take action. Self-confidence is an essential trait, and a worthy quality to encourage in others.

AFFIRMATION: I am balanced, focused, and confident.

Day 3

Values

Values are your beliefs. They determine the way you think, and the choices you make. They are not materialistic things like new cars, jewelry, vacations, or designer labels. The values you choose should honor and inspire your spirit. Love, security, health, and family are important values to many people. You can also focus on spiritual enlightenment.

There is no correct and complete list of values. They are not common interests, like movies and tennis, but beliefs such as work, honesty, and kindness that bind people together. We set our standards by first establishing our values. Determine your top five values, then work to not compromise them, and they will guide you to fulfillment.

AFFIRMATION: I live my values.

Spirituality
Acceptance
Compassion
Family
Gratitude
Kindness
Abundance
Accomplishment
Self-Sufficient

Day 4
Emotions

Emotions are the way we express our feelings. They communicate our happiness, pain, anger, and love. They are as necessary to your well-being as breathing.

Emotions can frequently fluctuate up and down. The energy you provide them often determines your reaction in certain situations. Negative emotions like fear, anger, and depression create unhealthy results and impair progress. Taking time out to understand the true reason behind emotional upset provides an opportunity to see the larger picture, and reach a more productive conclusion.

Mastering emotions like love, compassion, and patience gives you personal power. Before you fly off the handle, take ten seconds to consider the situation. Good communication, creativity, and wholesome relationships are important to your emotional well-being.

AFFIRMATION: I master my emotions.

Day 5

Responsibility

Responsibility means being accountable, making clear and rational decisions, and taking meaningful action. Irresponsibility manifests when people procrastinate and blame others for their misfortunes and mistakes. Avoid being a finger-pointer.

When you make a mistake own up to it; take immediate steps to amend it. Learning from your mistakes helps you to make better choices and claim responsibility.

Rather than complain, shoulder your obligations. Acknowledge that you are responsible for your behavior. Love and nurture your relationships and honor your commitments to yourself and others. Embracing your responsibility helps you manifest your dreams and expands your personal and professional power.

AFFIRMATION: I am responsible for my thoughts and actions.

Day 6

Integrity

Integrity helps define character, credibility, and honor. When faced with a dilemma, it is tempting to seek a quick and easy answer. Instead, you must ask yourself if there is a moral message in your predicament.

Everyone faces the consequences of their actions sooner or later. Whatever the situation, did you give it your full attention? Were you completely honest? Did you blame someone else? Or were you forthright in all your affairs, claiming responsibility for each and every action?

Being of sound moral principle is not always easy and often requires more effort than we believe we can give. Let integrity guide your conscience and design your code of ethics.

AFFIRMATION: I have integrity in all situations.

Day 7

Meditation

Meditation is a calm state of relaxation that creates spiritual and physical well-being. Begin by meditating three times a week for ten or fifteen minutes at a time. Once the process becomes more natural, you will want to meditate more often to help release stress and restore energy.

To begin, turn off all the distractions in your space and clear your mind. Find a comfortable chair, light a scented candle, and play soft music or a guided meditation CD. Close your eyes, breathe deeply, relax your body and invite serenity to settle over you.

Meditation is a quiet reflection to help you reach within and bring harmony and healing into your life. Meditation promotes intuition and attracts the knowledge to help you make better decisions. Meditate often because it heightens your total awareness and spiritual enlightenment.

AFFIRMATION: I meditate for inner peace and wisdom.

Day 8

Health

Good health heightens your passion and enthusiasm for life. Like a cocoon that houses a beautiful butterfly, your body shelters your soul. If you abuse your body with a poor diet, addiction, or excessive stress, you injure your soul as well. Depression, anger, and even lack of self-esteem can result.

Focus on ways to nurture your health. Drink plenty of water to rid your body of toxins and aid digestion. Avoid eating junk food that can clog the pathways to vital organs. You want to stay heart-healthy. Remember what Mom said about eating plenty of fresh fruits and vegetables? She was right. Your body needs a reliable supply of vitamins and minerals to keep your brain and organs in good working order to prevent disease.

Mark your calendar every year for your dental check-up and a doctor visit. Establish clear communication with your doctors so you are committed to a healthy regimen. You're worth it.

AFFIRMATION: I am healthy in body, mind, and spirit.

Day 9

Exercise

The more you exercise, the stronger and more confident you'll feel. Choose an activity that suits your needs and temperament. Even if you have a back problem, a brisk walk or a refreshing swim can be an excellent and safe aerobic exercise. Commit to your exercise on a regular basis. No excuses. Just do it! It isn't necessary to become a long-distance runner or seek the perfect body.

If you lack motivation, work out with a friend who can boost your involvement and solidify your sense of commitment. Exercise relieves stress and keeps you focused. It boosts your quality of life and longevity. Consider aerobics, hiking, biking, weightlifting, swimming, golf, or yoga. Get your body moving, do something wonderful for yourself, and keep healthy. It's never too late to start an exercise program. Today is the day.

AFFIRMATION: I commit to exercise each week.

Day 10
Balance

Having balance in your personal and professional life brings you stability and satisfaction. Balance is essential to create inner harmony and symmetry with the people around you.

For most people, there are eight important facets to life: family, social, physical, education, professional, financial, attitude, and spiritual. The challenge is to maintain healthy proportions in each area.

Like dominoes, if you are out of balance in one or more areas, there will be a chain reaction affecting your entire well-being. For example, if you do not engage in regular physical exercise, it will impact your attitude at work because you'll lack energy and won't have an outlet to burn off your stress.

When you're out of balance, immediately take measures to correct the imbalance by putting more time and energy into those areas being neglected. Staying positive and being aware are the first steps in maintaining a healthy balance.

AFFIRMATION: I create balance in my life.

Day 11

Relationships

The ability to communicate and interact with others is vital to establishing healthy relationships. As with your roles in life, your relationships will vary depending upon circumstances. For example, we connect with ourselves, God, family, friends, and even pets. There are many levels of relationships, some close and interactive, and others more impersonal.

Your goal is to instill harmony, cooperation, and real values into your relationships. Respect your differences, treat people as you wish to be treated, and avoid judgment. Above all, be honest with yourself and others. Let down your barriers, conquer fear, laugh, cry, love, and prosper. Form lasting bonds with those you care about.

AFFIRMATION: I have positive relationships.

Day 12

Humor

Laughter is a wonderful way to bring serenity to the soul. Seeing the humor in stressful situations helps you to laugh at yourself and lighten your mood. When circumstances don't go your way, relieve your frustration with humor.

Humor diminishes anger. Think about how you feel in a tense situation when someone cracks a joke at just the right time and the tension dissipates. It's fun to be around people who are upbeat and lighthearted. Science has proven that the more humor and laughter you enjoy in your life, the longer and healthier you'll live.

AFFIRMATION: I laugh easily and often.

Day 13

Inner Peace

When you awaken each morning you can choose to set your mood for the day. Sure, there will be situations that irritate you, but you can elect to not let them control your attitude and demeanor. Inner peace is a state of mind that you can develop through meditation, by calming your thoughts and connecting with your spirit.

Rid yourself of anger, judgment, and prejudice, for these negative thoughts destroy your potential for serenity. Inner peace is a virtue you can develop and nurture.

To create inner peace, take a few deep breaths, focus on what is really important, and wait for a calm feeling before speaking or acting. Replace negative thoughts with loving and affirming ones to help improve your peaceful attitude.

AFFIRMATION: I manifest inner peace.

Day 14

Spirituality

On a daily basis, trust your inner voice and your relationship with God to guide and enlighten you. Spirituality gives you awareness and fulfillment. If it is your wish to mature spiritually, seek ways to enhance your inner contentment. Your spirit also connects you with nature.

The definition of spirituality is that which relates to the human soul as opposed to material or physical things. Prayer is how you ask for help or guidance. Meditation is the way you listen for the answer. Owning spirituality is to exist at a higher level of awareness. You can help friends or neighbors in need, become active in your child's school, volunteer for a charity, or work in a local hospital. By combining worldly acts of kindness with spiritual energy, you acquire purpose and fulfillment.

AFFIRMATION: I am a spiritual being.

Day 15

Purpose

Purpose is the burning desire fueling the pursuit of a goal you wish to accomplish. It may be inspired by family, career, health, a sport, emotional or financial goals and may change during different stages of your life.

An Olympic hopeful's purpose maybe to qualify for the team and earn one or more medals. Some parents aspire to pass certain qualities on to their children, such as self-reliance and love. Others find great reward in community service or building a church, and some see their purpose as creating financial abundance.

Enjoy today, but take time to revitalize your purpose; give thought as to why and where you want to be. Defining and then pursuing a worthy purpose will empower you to manifest greater rewards than you could ever imagine.

AFFIRMATION: I live with purpose.

Day 16

Work

Your work should create a sense of usefulness and accomplishment, along with financial reward. If you dislike your work, it becomes drudgery and steals your time and health. When work brings you enjoyment, you're creative and happy. Whatever work you do, embrace the experience and insights you gather along the way. Choose a career you like and go for it!

Remember, everything you learn has the potential to benefit you with your next endeavor. A waiter could run his own restaurant. A teacher may become a great motivator and change hundreds of lives. Be willing to take risks to discover the work you are destined to do.

AFFIRMATION: I enjoy my work.

Day 17

Knowledge

It's exciting to learn! Knowledge can enhance experience and build awareness. Seek out effective ways of expanding your knowledge through classes, CDs, books, the internet, or other people's expertise. Broaden your skill set by tackling a language, craft, volunteer activity, or computer class.

Informed citizens acquire knowledge that can empower them in protecting injustice, judgment, and discrimination. Seeking knowledge opens the mind to explore challenging new situations and possibilities. In difficult situations, knowledge gives you the leverage to make intelligent decisions.

Whether you're fifteen or seventy-five, knowledge empowers your choices. Make it a lifelong pursuit and a legacy to pass on to others.

AFFIRMATION: I expand my mind through knowledge.

Day 18

Communication

Communication covers how we express ourselves and receive information from others. There is no greater skill to build your confidence and move you up the career ladder than knowing what to say and how to say it.

Unfortunately, people spend less time developing their communication skills than they do watching their favorite television programs. When you communicate openly with family, friends, and co-workers, you encourage honest and fulfilling relationships. Be candid and positive, and speak and write with honesty and commitment.

Be a good listener by inviting people to express themselves and share information. Interactive communication encourages an exchange of thoughts and ideas that focus on solutions.

AFFIRMATION: I am an effective communicator.

Day 19

Consciousness

Consciousness is a state of awareness of one's thoughts and feelings. Higher levels of consciousness unite your soul with purpose, integrity, and virtue. Increasing your awareness helps you connect more effectively with other people. Consciousness promotes empathy, patience, tolerance, forgiveness, and understanding.

When searching for solutions, allow your consciousness to heighten your awareness and focus your attention on the highest good. Perception, alertness, kindness, sensitivity, emotional maturity, and thoughtfulness are all traits of a heightened spiritual consciousness.

AFFIRMATION: I trust my consciousness to enlighten me.

Day 20

Vision

To develop your vision, take a few moments each morning and evening to clearly visualize what you want and who you want to be. Through your daily meditations and affirmations, you can confirm what you ask for: health, abundance, adventure, and love. Feel, believe, and see your future. Ask if it is for your highest good. Live in the present with gratitude, and believe you are manifesting your vision. Through the power of visualization and dedication, you can become be an accomplished golfer, a great parent, or a business owner.

Envision your goals and impress them into your heart and mind. Then develop an action plan to make them real. Let your intuition guide you. Imagine what you want, be clear on why you want it, and then take action.

AFFIRMATION: I visualize the life I desire.

Day 21

Abundance

Abundance surrounds you and can be attracted to you in many different ways. Being thankful for all that you have rather than focusing on what you don't will help you keep a positive outlook. Your work and your expression of appreciation help manifest abundance.

You may believe the party is somewhere else when it's actually happening right now with you. People aren't born to live in poverty, but to love and live in joy, and to help one another do the same. Take a good look around and really see all that surrounds you. Do you have shelter, food, freedom of speech, libraries, and schools? Be thankful for your friends, family, pets, and all the blessings in your life. Be sure to thank the Universe for giving you the opportunity to work for what you want.

Abundance exists on all levels—financial, emotional, spiritual, and mental. Believe you are worthy of abundance and welcome it into your heart.

AFFIRMATION: I create abundance.

Day 22

Passion

*Do what you love and believe in who you are. It's your passion that
ignites the energy to move from thought to action. Martin Luther King,
Jr., Louis Pasteur, and Mother Teresa were passionate people who believed
in their work, and their dedication altered history. Let them serve as role
models; live and love with boundless enthusiasm.*

*Are you committed to your relationships, work, and a healthy lifestyle?
If not, take a long hard look at what is holding you back from realizing your
desires. Is fear from your past preventing you from kindling the fires of
passion? If so, let go of the past and live in the present. What do you want in
your life? Go for it now. Every day is a new adventure. Live each one with
gusto.*

AFFIRMATION: I live with passion.

Day 23

Family

When you interact with your family, treat them with gentleness, kindness, respect, and love. A loving family environment provides a safe haven where you can belong. It's a place of refuge where hugs are plentiful, common interests are shared, and feelings are talked through.

When the outside world becomes lonely and fragmented, we turn to our family for comfort, safety, and understanding. We benefit from shared wisdom, resources, and support. If you make a mistake or are harsh, apologize. Keep the lines of communication open. No one is perfect. Sometimes it is difficult but be forgiving and accepting. Unconditional love and deep bonding are the rare gifts a family can give.

AFFIRMATION: I love my family.

Day 24

Compassion

Compassion is a pure form of emotion. It heals relationships, raises self-esteem, and is a caring legacy to pass on from generation to generation. When you are compassionate, you identify with others from deep within yourself.

Being compassionate means listening when a friend is going through a tough time and being patient when someone has difficulty making a decision. Looking beyond your own needs and being of service to others is one of the greatest comforts you can give to another living being.

Practicing empathy awakens your heart and soul to the boundless joy of spiritual awareness. Although extremely challenging at times, it is well worth the effort to practice acts of kindness and compassion.

AFFIRMATION: I am compassionate.

Day 25

Persistence

Persistence is having the tenacity to move forward through obstacles and disappointments. It is often the difference between failure and success. Many people fall short in their lives because they do not open their hearts and minds to the gifts of inner strength and perseverance.

Sales studies indicate it takes five or more interactions to make a sale, yet many people give up after the first rejection. Persistence makes the difference between drafting an outline of a book and publishing it, or taking a few classes and earning a degree. You could hit a few tennis balls or you could become an excellent tennis player. It takes practice and persistence.

When you believe in yourself, abundance and fulfillment follow. Being persistent expands your confidence and helps you achieve your dreams.

AFFIRMATION: I am persistent.

Day 26

Change

Confronting change means overcoming your fears and taking action. Change is an opportunity to stretch yourself and grow beyond your comfort zone. Change does not guarantee you will be successful in all your endeavors, but is an ever-present dynamic you must learn to accept.

Choosing to live a life of quiet desperation filled with fear of change keeps you forever wondering what life would be like if only you had tried something different. Four of the saddest words are, "I should have tried."

The challenge to change and grow as an individual can lead to very rewarding experiences. Although sometimes scary and seemingly insurmountable, change is often forced upon you, but the benefit of taking on transformation is spiritual growth.

Look forward with self-respect and confidence toward what you will accomplish.

AFFIRMATION: I embrace change as an opportunity.

Day 27

Creativity

Your creativity is an expression of your originality. It is your unique imagination that makes your dreams and desires come alive. Have the courage to explore your creative potential and expand its boundaries through training, coaching, and education. Who knows, you might possess the qualities to become a master painter or perfect a family recipe and turn it into a successful business. The sky is the limit.

How do you discover your creativity? Relax in a quiet place, close your eyes, unwind, and allow your stream of consciousness to go to work. Think about what you like to do, what inspires you and brings you joy. Jot your ideas down and open up your imagination to all the possibilities life offers.

Focus on one or two talents you enjoy. Visualize yourself following through by purchasing the supplies, signing up for a class, or designing a space where you can bring your world of ideas to life. Then, commit energy and time to express your talents. Creativity enriches your life.

AFFIRMATION: I am creative.

Day 28

Manifestation

Manifestation is the ability to attract what you desire in life. By determining what you want to manifest and clarifying if it is for your highest good, you can outline your goals. The ideal way to begin the process is through meditation. Calm yourself in a quiet place, light a candle, play soft music or listen to a guided CD, and ask to connect to a higher source.

In your quiet state of mind, explore what it is that brings you joy and best serves your highest purpose. Take note of the answer that comes to you. Once you know what you want, focus on it and visualize your life as though you already have it. You may manifest a home, fulfillment in a career, or a loving relationship with your child. Then, work for it. Most importantly, be grateful for what you have and what is yet to come to you.

Using the skills of visualization and self-talk, remember that is saying or thinking positive thoughts, will draw to you what you desire. God didn't put you on the earth to suffer. Live with purpose and attract what you want through manifestation.

AFFIRMATION: I manifest my highest good.

Day 29
Love

Love is a deep, tender feeling of affection that allows you to express compassion and tenderness. You first must love yourself to be able to love others. Always know that God loves you as you are. Be more patient and tolerant of yourself.

True love demonstrates emotional and mature growth. When you genuinely love someone, you encourage them to be all they can be. We gain insight from different kinds of love: romantic love, love for parents, siblings, children, friends, and love of oneself.

When you have love, it adds value to your life; you're healthier, less stressed, more confident and you open your life to kindness, friendship, and laughter. Love without judgment. Love is the greatest commitment we can make to the Universe, ourselves, and others.

AFFIRMATION: I love unconditionally.

Day 30

Life

Life encompasses the spiritual, mental, and physical experiences of your existence. Every day brings newness. The quality of your life is determined by the choices you make, the people you associate with, and the knowledge you gain from your experiences. Circumstances and situations in life are not always fair, but you are in control of how you allow these things to affect your attitude and values. By focusing on your appreciation of family and friends and consistently expressing gratitude, you will create a meaningful life.

We all face obstacles and challenges from time to time. It's how you react that determines the outcome. You are an individual like no other. You maintain your own set of fingerprints and no one else has your biography. You have been gifted with special talents to benefit yourself and others. Life is an opportunity for you to contribute to the world—become a teacher, volunteer, mentor, nurse, an inventor, or whatever your calling may be. The important thing is to explore your potential and grow your talents. The reward for your efforts will be an abundant life. Live in the moment. Love, laugh, and live your destiny.

AFFIRMATION: I live each day to the fullest.

Fire Up Series

In these uncertain times, the human spirit yearns for hope and enlightenment so each of us may survive and thrive. The **Fire Up** series recounts a compelling true-life journey, delivering timely inspiration along with timeless wisdom. Donna Hartley is crowned Miss Hawaii and her attention is captured by a kind and patient soul, George, who mysteriously prophesies that her success is paved with learning lessons. He relates to her in storytelling form that Donna must survive three life-threatening events if she is to fulfill her destiny. Is George a wise man, a mentor, an angel, or all three?

Fire Up Your Life! recounts Donna's near-death experience in a DC-10 plane crash at Los Angeles International Airport, which occurs directly after she expresses her desire to change her life or die. Trapped in the flaming inferno, she receives a mysterious message questioning her actions on earth. She wills herself to survive and is the last passenger out of her section of the aircraft. With the steadfast help of her teacher George, the reluctant student Donna begins a journey of spiritual transformation committing herself to change her fearful and unhealthy lifestyle. Her first assignment is to fight for improved airline safety regulations. Next, she must conquer her destructive relationships with men. Moreover, to become a successful entrepreneur she must master her fears.

Fire Up Your Intuition! finds Donna distraught in an emotional and financial crisis. George unexpectedly appears and bestows on her five mysterious envelopes that hold a 30-day assignment that he calls "the gift of intuition." The banter and discussion continue between student and teacher as Donna works to acquire insight into her own intuitive awareness. Her faithful Himalayan cat Sheba is by her side as Donna follows George's program step by step to learn to trust her feelings and act upon them to master *the knowing.* George predicts that when she completes her assignment, her dream to adopt a daughter will come true.

Fire Up Your Healing! narrates the sometimes rocky path on the passage toward family forgiveness leading to emotional maturity and the strength to heal. Donna travels from the tragic confines of her mother's post-stroke nursing home to the somber quarters of the judge empowered with deciding the fate for the bitter court battle in which her stepmother has embroiled Donna and her brother upon their father's death. George adamantly advises her to release her anger in order to survive. Could she forgive the alcoholism, the violence, and the indifference? This skill is now essential if she is to survive her stage III melanoma. But can she forgive herself and live to raise her six-year-old daughter? George mystically appears in the hospital to give Donna a shot of spiritual adrenalin and the courage to face down the deadly disease.

Fire Up Your Heart! begins at the gravesite of her stepdad as a heartbroken Donna deals with the eleventh death of family and friends in the past few years. Her nagging intuition forces her to consult a heart specialist and the prognosis is her worst fear: she must have immediate open-heart surgery to replace her failing aortic valve. Her daughter Mariah, now age ten, is the driving force to help her live. Donna's friends rally to lend her support for the delicate surgery scheduled for **March 1,** the same date of her plane crash and melanoma diagnosis. What are those chances? Donna must summon all her strength and hard-won wisdom to survive. Will George spiritually guide her through this life-threatening operation? Has Donna learned her lessons so she can cheat death for the third time?

CPSIA information can be obtained at www.ICGtesting.com
Printed in the USA
LVOW06s2027040813

346179LV00002B/90/P

9 781935 953166